New Day

Edited by **Sally Welch**   January–April 2020

The BRF Prayer

Almighty God,
you have taught us that your word is a lamp for our feet
and a light for our path. Help us, and all who prayerfully
read your word, to deepen our fellowship with you
and with each other through your love.
And in so doing may we come to know you more fully,
love you more truly, and follow more faithfully
in the steps of your Son Jesus Christ, who lives and reigns
with you and the Holy Spirit, one God forevermore.
Amen

We want to hear from you!

Complete our short survey for the chance to win a FREE subscription!
Let us know what you like about BRF's Bible reading notes
and how we can improve them to help more people
encounter God through the Bible.

Go to **brfonline.org.uk/BRNSURVEY**

Making disciples of all nations

In the coming days we will be thinking about the final instructions that Jesus gave to his disciples as recorded in Matthew 28:19–20. The eleven disciples were caught in a whirlpool of emotion after the harrowing death of their master and his subsequent astounding resurrection. Jesus instructs them to make their way back to their homeland of Galilee and to climb a mountain. There, on that lofty mountain, they meet with their risen Lord. They stand on this high place, overlooking the land spread out before them. Jesus stretches his arm to the far distance and gives them their marching orders: 'Go... and make disciples of all nations' (v. 19, NRSV). The Greek word for 'nation' is *ethnos*, from which we get our word 'ethnic'. In the New Testament, 'the nations' is also often used as a term for all the Gentiles. The eleven are to go to the multitude of different cultures and ethnic groups across the globe, both Jew and Gentile, and proclaim the good news of Jesus and baptise new disciples.

Quite how those eleven took to the news of this commission is hard to know, but we do know they were no less human than you or me, and they probably found the task pretty daunting. Their training was over, and the serious work was now beginning. However, their nerves are steadied by the wonderful promise of Jesus: 'I am with you always' (v. 20). Matthew begins his gospel by telling us that Jesus is Emmanuel – 'God is with us' (1:23). He closes his gospel with the same message.

For the disciples, this mountaintop moment marks the beginning of a new story – the missionary story. At the beginning of this new year, we look at how Jesus reached out to different peoples with the gospel and made disciples and at how the first disciples followed his example. When Jesus pointed to the far distance from that mountain, he was pointing across time as well as space – thus the good news has reached us, and we, too, are summoned to follow the call. In the coming days, we shall have a look at some stories that tell us what this making disciples of all nations means.

MICHAEL MITTON

Early clues

When they had heard the king, they set out; and there, ahead of them, went the star that they had seen at its rising, until it stopped over the place where the child was. When they saw that the star had stopped, they were overwhelmed with joy. On entering the house, they saw the child with Mary his mother; and they knelt down and paid him homage. Then, opening their treasure-chests, they offered him gifts of gold, frankincense, and myrrh.

Our first story takes us back to the birth of Jesus and the visit of the magi. We are approaching the feast of Epiphany, when traditionally we remember this curious story, which occurred when Jesus was still little. Nothing could have prepared Mary and Joseph for this impressive entourage that arrived unheralded at their door. Matthew tells us the magi came 'from the East' (2:1). As frankincense and myrrh were harvested from trees in southern Arabia, it is reckoned that these men came from there.

Mary and Joseph were devout Jews and presumably held the conventional view of the day that Gentiles were generally to be regarded as unclean and should not enter the house of a Jew. But these parents of Jesus saw beyond such restricted religious views and welcomed them into their home. As they watched these eastern visitors pay homage to their little boy, they must have seen this as early evidence that the good news wrapped up in the life of their child was for all people, regardless of race or creed. Even pagan astrologers from far-off lands could have open hearts and eyes to discover the Christ. The magi alert us to the wonderful truth that there are people all over the world who have not yet heard the good news but have developed eyes to see the signs of God. Sometimes it may be the people we least expect. Part of the missionary call is to search out such people, so that we may lead them to the God they long to worship. Furthermore, they may have spotted things about the kingdom that we have failed to see.

Who do you think are the equivalent of the magi today?

MICHAEL MITTON

Faith in surprising places

'But the truth is, there were many widows in Israel in the time of Elijah, when the heaven was shut up for three years and six months, and there was a severe famine over all the land; yet Elijah was sent to none of them except to a widow at Zarephath in Sidon. There were also many lepers in Israel in the time of the prophet Elisha, and none of them was cleansed except Naaman the Syrian.' When they heard this, all in the synagogue were filled with rage.

After the infancy narratives, Luke tells us about the baptism of Jesus followed by his testing in the wilderness, after which Jesus begins his public ministry. Jesus returns to his home town of Nazareth, and Luke provides us with his first recorded sermon. As it turns out, the sermon nearly gets him thrown off a cliff!

There is some discussion as to what it was that shocked that synagogue. One likely possibility is Jesus' choice of two historical characters to demonstrate powerful faith. He explains that at the time of Elijah there were many widows in Israel. God could have sent Elijah to any of them, but instead the one who caught his eye was a widow who lived in Sidon, a land that worshipped Baal. Similarly, in the time of Elisha, there were many lepers who were of the correct religion, but the person God chose to heal was the pagan Naaman. In other words, God bypassed the people with the right religious credentials and honoured two Gentiles. It was perhaps this that enflamed that prim and proper synagogue: they might have thought that if Jesus was going to preach a sermon on impressive faith, why choose two unworthy Gentiles rather than the accepted heroes of faith, such as Abraham or David? Such teaching, they may have felt, was subversive and would destabilise their world view that God had his favourites to whom he gave special privileges.

Jesus escapes his accusers and in the next three years he regularly shows that God does not favour a privileged few. What he looks for is vibrant, humble faith, no matter where it resides.

What does this sermon of Jesus say to you about how we make disciples?

MICHAEL MITTON

Jesus' choice of disciples

As he walked by the Sea of Galilee, he saw two brothers, Simon, who is called Peter, and Andrew his brother, casting a net into the lake – for they were fishermen. And he said to them, 'Follow me, and I will make you fish for people.' Immediately they left their nets and followed him. As he went from there, he saw two other brothers, James son of Zebedee and his brother John, in the boat with their father Zebedee, mending their nets, and he called them. Immediately they left the boat and their father, and followed him.

The ruler of that synagogue in Nazareth, from yesterday's reading, might have preferred today's story to run something like this: 'As he walked by the Sea of Galilee, Jesus saw a highly qualified rabbi studying his Pentateuch. And he said, "Follow me and I will make you found a training school for religious teachers." As he went on from there, Jesus saw two brothers, both scribes who were learned in the law, and he called them. Immediately they followed him.'

However, that was not Jesus' way. He had lived 30 years on this earth by now and had had a good chance to study humankind. He needed to find twelve teachable people to form his first discipleship group. Even though we may be so familiar with this, it can still be a little surprising that the first people he chose were Peter, who seems to get quite a bit wrong, particularly at the crucial time of Jesus' trial, and James and John, whom Jesus nicknames 'sons of thunder', suggesting they had some emotional volatility. These two also suffered from illusions of grandeur (Mark 10:37). We know in the end these men turned out to be remarkable disciples and disciple-makers, but at the beginning the material Jesus was working with was pretty raw. However, Jesus viewed humanity with very different eyes from most. He saw not only what people were but what they could become. Sometimes the first stage of disciple-making is prayerfully discerning what someone might become when their hearts are touched by grace. We then watch as that grace takes effect.

Lord, give me the eyes to see not just the person but who they can become.

MICHAEL MITTON

Making disciples: the Samaritan

A Samaritan woman came to draw water, and Jesus said to her, 'Give me a drink'. (His disciples had gone to the city to buy food.) The Samaritan woman said to him, 'How is it that you, a Jew, ask a drink of me, a woman of Samaria?' (Jews do not share things in common with Samaritans.) Jesus answered her, 'If you knew the gift of God, and who it is that is saying to you, "Give me a drink", you would have asked him, and he would have given you living water.'

In this story, Jesus breaks two major conventions – one religious and the other social. It is well known that there was deep hostility between Jews and Samaritans, but John gives this story a prominent place in his gospel, as he is in no doubt that the gospel transcends these racial, religious and gender divides that are formed by human pride and fear.

Jesus is sitting by a well in Samaria – he is comfortable in this land that is supposed to be enemy territory. The woman approaches, and they engage in conversation. Jesus shows no discomfort at the fact that she is a Samaritan nor at her string of broken marriages and her current domestic arrangement. The woman shows she is not one for being bound by social conventions, because she is quite comfortable arguing with this travelling rabbi from Galilee.

The conversation is brought to an end by the arrival of the disciples, who are shocked to see their master on his own in the company of a woman. She departs to her hometown, where she tells the people that Jesus 'told me everything I have ever done' (John 4:29). Of all the things that took place in that conversation, it was Jesus' loving acceptance of her life story that touched her most. And it touched her neighbours, too, for they invite Jesus into their town and, at the end of his stay, they declare he 'is truly the Saviour of the world' (John 4:42). Jesus, ignoring religious and social conventions, stepped into an alien culture and listened to a person's story. The human divisions soon dissolved, and many came to faith.

What might the equivalent of a Samaritan be for you today?

MICHAEL MITTON

Making disciples: the Roman

When he entered Capernaum, a centurion came to him, appealing to him and saying, 'Lord, my servant is lying at home paralysed, in terrible distress.' And he said to him, 'I will come and cure him.' The centurion answered, 'Lord, I am not worthy to have you come under my roof; but only speak the word, and my servant will be healed. For I also am a man under authority, with soldiers under me...' When Jesus heard him, he was amazed and said to those who followed him, 'Truly I tell you, in no one in Israel have I found such faith.'

In his sermon in the Nazareth synagogue (Luke 4), Jesus commended two Old Testament Gentiles for their faith. The hero of today's story is an equivalent in the ministry of Jesus. Centurions were regarded as the finest soldiers in the Roman army. Interestingly every centurion mentioned in the New Testament is associated with honour.

The centurion in today's story is clearly an exceptional man. First, he treats his servant (slave) with affection, which was very unusual in the Roman world, where most slaves were treated as things rather than people. Second, though Jesus offers to come to his house, he shows remarkable respect for the customs of the Jews, whose laws would not allow them to enter Gentile homes. Third, and most impressively, this centurion understood that the earthly dynamics of power and authority could be applied in the spiritual realm. He commanded soldiers to go; Jesus commanded diseases to flee. Jesus spent much time trying to teach his disciples this; the centurion had worked it out for himself. And Jesus declared he had never seen such faith in all of Israel.

We naturally expect faith to run high in our church communities, because that is where our discipleship is nurtured. However, we have to acknowledge that sometimes it is people way beyond the confines of our church who understand the dynamics of faith, at times even better than us. Such people often have the qualities of kindness and humility seen in our centurion. Sometimes God uses the most surprising people to be our tutors in the dynamics of faith.

Lord, lead me to those who will help my faith to grow.

MICHAEL MITTON

Making disciples: the foreigner

From there he set out and went away to the region of Tyre… A woman whose little daughter had an unclean spirit immediately heard about him, and she came and bowed down at his feet. Now the woman was a Gentile, of Syrophoenician origin. She begged him to cast the demon out of her daughter. He said to her, 'Let the children be fed first, for it is not fair to take the children's food and throw it to the dogs.' But she answered him, 'Sir, even the dogs under the table eat the children's crumbs.' Then he said to her, 'For saying that, you may go – the demon has left your daughter.'

Jesus takes a fascinating excursion with his disciples into the Gentile territory of Phoenicia, and it is here that he intends to take a quiet retreat. However, even in this world beyond Galilee and Judea, news is spreading about this intriguing rabbi who can perform miracles. Thus it is that a desperate mother discovers where Jesus is staying, and she comes to him and begs for his help with her daughter. Jesus' response to her seems discourteous in the extreme. For a start, he seems to offer a blunt refusal to help, and then he insults her by implying that she and her daughter are no better than dogs. 'Dog' was a derogatory term for a Gentile. Impressively, the woman is not deterred. Her response demonstrates to Jesus that she is a woman of humility and faith, and once again he performs a remote healing.

Remarkably, what we have in this story is a Gentile woman apparently changing Jesus' mind: Jesus clearly denies her the healing, but her response so impresses him that he does heal her daughter. He caught sight of the character of this woman the moment she stepped in the door and he perceived that by provoking her, he would bring the best out in her. Rather than being offended, she turns his insult into an opportunity for sharing her wisdom. Jesus loved to find such sparks of life and faith and used every opportunity to draw it out of people. He delighted to find such confident faith in this foreigner.

What do you learn from this story?

MICHAEL MITTON

A message for all nations

Amazed and astonished, they asked, 'Are not all these who are speaking Galileans? And how is it that we hear, each of us, in our own native language? Parthians, Medes, Elamites, and residents of Mesopotamia, Judea and Cappadocia, Pontus and Asia, Phrygia and Pamphylia, Egypt and the parts of Libya belonging to Cyrene, and visitors from Rome, both Jews and proselytes, Cretans and Arabs – in our own languages we hear them speaking about God's deeds of power.'

After Jesus had given his commission to the disciples, he ascended and left them to it. Despite his promise of power from on high, they must have wondered quite how they would make disciples of all nations. But then comes the feast of Pentecost and, as it happened, 'every nation under heaven' (Acts 2:5) gathered to Jerusalem for this festival. As the disciples pray together, the Spirit is released upon them. The consequence of this remarkable visitation is an immediate fulfilment of Jesus' command: the wind of God blows the disciples out on to the streets, where each one finds he or she is speaking fluently in another language. Following Peter's sermon, 3,000 people are baptised. The disciples realise that, with this gift of the Spirit, the great commission is not as daunting as they thought.

Among the many vital messages of this Pentecost story stands one that is very significant for our times: that is, if we are to make disciples of people from cultures different from our own, then we need the inspiration of God to help us understand their language – not just the language of their lips, but also the language of their hearts. It is fascinating to think that those early Christian groups spoke in so many different languages – the gospel found a natural home in each.

Sadly, too often we expect those who are different from us to learn *our* language and culture and to conform to *our* way of doing things. The Pentecost story reveals a more generous way, which is learning the ways of the other and respecting their culture. A missional church will look culturally much like the people the church is trying to reach and will be learning their language.

Send me out, O Lord, in the power of your Spirit.

MICHAEL MITTON

Making disciples: the Ethiopian

Now there was an Ethiopian eunuch, a court official of the Candace, queen of the Ethiopians, in charge of her entire treasury. He had come to Jerusalem to worship and was returning home; seated in his chariot, he was reading the prophet Isaiah. Then the Spirit said to Philip, 'Go over to this chariot and join it.' So Philip ran up to it and heard him reading the prophet Isaiah. He asked, 'Do you understand what you are reading?' He replied, 'How can I, unless someone guides me?' And he invited Philip to get in and sit beside him.

This Ethiopian official is a good example of someone from 'every nation under heaven' who visited Jerusalem for a festival. Philip happens to be in the area when he sees an official-looking party journeying to the coast. Philip has learned that effective missionary endeavour comes from a divine prompt. As far as we know, he was not working from a training manual for evangelism and discipleship. He just happens to be alert and open to God's Spirit, and it is God's Spirit who points him to the chariot and effectively says, 'I need you there.' When Philip gets to the chariot, he hears the Ethiopian reading the prophet Isaiah, so Philip knows this man is in the mood to think about God. Perhaps one of the best missional texts we have is 'he invited Philip to get in and sit beside him' (v. 31). Philip's evangelism is in response to both a prompting of God and an invitation from the person to sit in their carriage. Philip does not say, 'Stop this carriage and come with me to my church.' He stays with the flow of what God has already started in this African heart, and it is not long before the two are standing in a desert pool with Philip splashing baptismal waters over his new friend; the waters of life are now released in the nation of Ethiopia.

Philip teaches us that disciple-making starts with our willingness to join someone's journey and respond to their questions as we go along. Such a way may feel very vulnerable, but God has given us the gift of his Spirit for just such occasions.

What does Philip's story say to you today?

MICHAEL MITTON

The open heart

As they were leaving, Paul made one further statement: 'The Holy Spirit was right in saying to your ancestors through the prophet Isaiah, "Go to this people and say, You will indeed listen, but never understand, and you will indeed look, but never perceive. For this people's heart has grown dull, and their ears are hard of hearing, and they have shut their eyes; so that they might not look with their eyes, and listen with their ears, and understand with their heart and turn – and I would heal them."'

The book of Acts is a collection of stories that describe how the first Christians faithfully followed the call of Jesus to make disciples of all nations. Led by Paul, they ventured out to the far corners of the Roman world carrying the gospel of Christ. In today's passage, we meet Paul, who is under house arrest in Rome. God's call to Paul was that he should preach the gospel to the Gentiles (Acts 9:15, where the word *ethnos* is used). He obeyed this call, but also always preached to his own people. However, in this passage he quotes the prophet Isaiah (a quote also used by Jesus in Matthew 13:13–15).

Jesus and Paul use this quote to convey the message that those who *should* be able to see the things of the kingdom often fail to – it is a warning to all of us who are established in our faith. Any heart can grow dull, and anyone can close their ears and eyes to the truth. Paul's heart was once so hard that he was intent on destroying those who proclaimed this kingdom. But then he had an extraordinary encounter with Christ that changed everything.

In whatever way we might find ourselves sharing the gospel and seeking to make disciples, the truth of the matter is that some will respond with open hearts and minds and others will remain stubbornly closed. It is not our job to force any heart open. Our job is to seek out the open hearts. Where we find closed hearts, the story of Paul reminds us that even the hardest heart can have extraordinary encounters with Christ.

Lord, soften my heart and keep my ears and eyes open.

MICHAEL MITTON

The power of the gospel

[Paul said:] 'Let it be known to you then that this salvation of God has been sent to the Gentiles; they will listen.' He lived there for two whole years at his own expense and welcomed all who came to him, proclaiming the kingdom of God and teaching about the Lord Jesus Christ with all boldness and without hindrance.

With these words, Luke brings Acts to a close. Some may feel that this is a curious place to finish – the great Paul under house arrest. But Luke is not writing a life of Paul. He is writing an account of what happens to people when the Spirit empowers them to proclaim the good news of Jesus. He starts with the story of Jesus promising his Spirit to his followers and how they will be his witnesses to the ends of the earth (1:8). The few followers have become tens of thousands. The story starts in Jerusalem and ends in Rome, the capital of the empire. Paul may be under house arrest, but from here he writes many of his letters, which still inspire disciples today. He welcomes many to his home and teaches about the kingdom of God. This imprisonment, far from impeding the gospel, is actually effecting its release to many.

Acts covers roughly the first 30 years of the church's response to Jesus' commission – to take the gospel to all nations. Despite all kinds of opposition and setbacks, in such a short space of time the Christian faith became a force to be reckoned with. There were remarkable people, like Paul, but much of the work was carried out by ordinary people who heard the news of an exceptional God and who received the Holy Spirit, who gave them the confidence to proclaim the kingdom of God to their friends and neighbours. We are the recipients of the same commission and the same Spirit. We may at times feel imprisoned and trapped by our own weakness, pressures in the church and the prevailing secularism of our age. But Luke, Paul and all those early pioneers of faith would remind us that there is a kingdom far stronger than any of these.

Lord Jesus, free me to be a faithful witness to your gospel today.

MICHAEL MITTON

All nations together in worship

After this I looked, and there before me was a great multitude that no one could count, from every nation, tribe, people and language, standing before the throne and before the Lamb. They were wearing white robes and were holding palm branches in their hands. And they cried out in a loud voice: 'Salvation belongs to our God, who sits on the throne, and to the Lamb.' All the angels were standing round the throne and round the elders and the four living creatures. They fell down on their faces before the throne and worshipped God.

The dramatic final book of the Bible is a record of a vision given to John, who is writing at the end of the first century. He has witnessed the gospel being proclaimed throughout the known world. In this vision, John is given insight into the glorious life of heaven, and in today's passage he recounts how he was privileged to see the worship of heaven – that is, worship in its purest form. One of the features of this perfect worship is the presence of every nation (*ethnos*), tribe, people and language, who are mingling with the angels in their worship of God. This vision of heavenly worship tells us that each and every people group is important to God. Not only that, but all these people groups find harmony together in such worship. The church is multicultural at its birth at Pentecost, and it is multicultural in heaven.

   This tells us that when we preach the gospel to all nations, there is a divine plan to bring those nations together in a new community that is not divided by race, nation or culture. Sadly, in the history of the church, this has been far from its experience. Humans all too easily find security in being among those who are the same. But the community of the Spirit is designed to be radically different. It was never designed to keep people out, but to welcome them in. Very often the people we find different or strange or with whom we disagree are the ones God uses to help us to grow as disciples of Christ.

How does this vision inspire you?

MICHAEL MITTON

Genesis 37—45: Joseph

We've probably known the thrilling story of Joseph since we were children. The long robe made by his indulgent father, the jealousy of his older brothers, vivid dreams, kidnap, slavery, escape and – the dramatic denouement – Joseph revealing himself as a powerful man who shames those who would have been rid of him. It's easy to remember the imagery of sheaves of corn bowing down to the sheaf gathered by Joseph, of the sun, moon and stars also bowing down, and of seven fat cows being eaten up by seven thin ones – dreams from God that give information about the future.

Yet look closer and it's a complex study of favouritism, rivalry and revenge. Jacob's family dynamics reflect the complications of inadequate parenting and multiple partners. The 13 children of his four different partners find themselves desperate to gain his attention, conscious that he loves Joseph most of all. Joseph himself is a fascinating character. Although at the beginning of the story he is 17 years old, he wanders through life as an innocent, putting himself into dangerous situations and speaking without any thought for the reactions his words will provoke. Perhaps he has been an overprotected younger child, kept safe from the harsh realities of the world. His mother, Rachel, died when giving birth to Benjamin, his little brother, and in such circumstances, it is easy to overcompensate. Perhaps Joseph's bluntness and painful honesty suggest difficulty with social interactions. He's certainly not, to begin with, someone who would be expected to rise to high rank in a foreign land.

Bible stories often act as a mirror, helping us to see aspects of ourselves in the behaviour of others. Jacob's 'blended family' is an extreme example of dysfunction, but most families will at some time struggle with sibling rivalries and shifting allegiances. Joseph speaks without thinking of the impact his words might cause; we all have done the same. And although kidnap, unjust imprisonment and slavery are unlikely to happen to most of us, they are still bitter realities for many people around the world. Joseph's story shows the working of God to bring something good out of something bad and the need, in dire circumstances, to hold on to faith and trust. In the end, all will be well.

AMANDA BLOOR

19

Telling tales

Joseph, being seventeen years old, was shepherding the flock with his brothers; he was a helper to the sons of Bilhah and Zilpah, his father's wives; and Joseph brought a bad report of them to their father. Now Israel loved Joseph more than any other of his children, because he was the son of his old age; and he had made him a long robe with sleeves. But when his brothers saw that their father loved him more than all his brothers, they hated him, and could not speak peaceably to him.

Joseph, at 17, should have known better than to tell tales about his brothers. But there can be rivalries within any family, and Jacob's was more complex than most. He had twelve sons and a daughter, born to his two wives and his wives' maids, and he did not hide the fact that Joseph was his favourite. The boy might have wanted to cement his position by undermining his older siblings, or it is possible that he was genuinely aggrieved by something they had done and complained without thinking of the consequences. Whatever his motivation, his actions set in motion a chain of events that he could never have foreseen.

However faithful we are, we are also human and there will be times when we are tempted to speak critically of others. Yet we never know the whole story. Perhaps we have clashed with someone who, like Joseph's brothers, is feeling neglected or overlooked. Perhaps the words or actions that offend us have been said or done lightly and carelessly, without serious intent. Perhaps we ourselves have hurt or annoyed others. 'Least said, soonest mended' is an old proverb that has much to commend it, as do the commandments to love our neighbour as ourselves and to forgive as generously as God forgives us.

We know, if we are honest, that there is much that each of us will regret having said throughout our lives. Can we pray that God will guide us to do better in the future?

Help me, Lord, to think before I speak and consider before I act. May I trust in your love for me so that I do not undermine or disparage others, knowing that you love them too.

AMANDA BLOOR

Hopes, fears and dreams

Once Joseph had a dream, and when he told it to his brothers, they hated him even more. He said to them, 'Listen to this dream that I dreamed. There we were, binding sheaves in the field. Suddenly my sheaf arose and stood upright; then your sheaves gathered around it, and bowed down to my sheaf.' His brothers said to him, 'Are you indeed to reign over us? Are you indeed to have dominion over us?'

I wonder what Joseph hoped to achieve when he told his dreams to his brothers? We might have thought that he would have learned discretion before speaking; after all, relationships with his siblings were already strained. Yet he described without reservation visions that could only be interpreted as showing his primacy over his family. In this dream his brothers' sheaves bow down to his, and in his next dream the sun, the moon and the stars bow down to him. Even Joseph's indulgent father was startled enough to rebuke the boy for his wild dreaming, although we are told that he 'kept the matter in mind'.

We all dream, although we don't always remember our dreams when we wake. Some dreams are more vivid than others and linger with us. The dreams that Joseph experienced, however, were so powerful that he was unable to hold back from sharing them with his family. In a culture where such visions were often interpreted as prophetic messages from God, he might have wondered if he was being granted a glimpse of the future. Would his father, mother and brothers really pay him obeisance? It's not easy to be the youngest in a large family. Perhaps Joseph hoped that by telling them the substance of his dreams, they would take him more seriously. Perhaps he wanted the dreams laughed away. Or perhaps he tried to understand what was happening to him – as many of us do – by talking it through.

Dear God, send us good advisers who can help us discern your action in our lives. Let us hear your calling and be ready to respond in faith and in trust.

AMANDA BLOOR

Fear and loathing

Then they took Joseph's robe, slaughtered a goat, and dipped the robe in the blood. They had the long robe with sleeves taken to their father, and they said, 'This we have found; see now whether it is your son's robe or not'… Then Jacob tore his garments, and put sackcloth on his loins, and mourned for his son for many days. All his sons and all his daughters sought to comfort him; but he refused to be comforted.

Poor Jacob! He must have struggled with the knowledge that it was he who had sent Joseph out into the wilderness, where – he believed – a wild animal had killed the boy. All those hours listening to his youngest son's stories and dreams, his hopes for the future, all destroyed along with that glorious robe, now a bloodstained remnant. The old man was appalled beyond all measure. 'I will be mourning until the day I die,' he cried.

The brothers, in contrast, seemed to be more concerned with keeping their secret than in offering consolation. How did they feel, I wonder, when they heard his weeping? Did they acknowledge their guilt or did this become another reason to blame Joseph for disrupting the family? After all, they might have reasoned, if he hadn't been such a sneak, they wouldn't have been forced to deal with him.

It must have been awful for all, with Jacob distraught and the brothers bearing a burden of knowledge that they had agreed to bury very deep. Yet whether through denial, in fear of the consequences or by justification of their actions, the brothers seem not to have thought of telling the truth. Jacob was a rich man and Egypt not too far away. If they had spoken up, Joseph might have been tracked down, bought back and returned home.

Backed into a corner by their own actions, the brothers chose to let two people – their brother and their father – suffer rather than reveal what they had done. Even Reuben, who tried to save Joseph, said nothing.

God, my strength and my salvation, keep me from the fear that paralyses and the loathing of self or others that leads to sinful actions. Fill me with your love.

AMANDA BLOOR

Starting again

The Lord was with Joseph, and he became a successful man; he was in the house of his Egyptian master. His master saw that the Lord was with him, and that the Lord caused all that he did to prosper in his hands. So Joseph found favour in his sight and attended him; he made him over-seer of his house and put him in charge of all that he had.

How do you begin again when the worst things you can imagine have happened? Joseph had to come to terms with the fact that his own siblings hated him so much that they nearly killed him before selling him into slavery, and he must have wondered why his father, who claimed to love him more than anyone else, hadn't come to his rescue. He was many miles away from the home where he'd been cherished and protected, in a strange country where he knew no one and where everything – language, customs, religious belief – was different. He must have been devastated.

Yet the young Israelite clearly stood out among other captive slaves. He was bought, probably for a good price, by one of Pharaoh's most trusted officers and was soon recognised as trustworthy and clever. Joseph became Potiphar's personal servant and was then put in charge of his house and farmlands. Treated as a servant rather than a slave, he had risen to an important position and used all his gifts to make his master's estate prosper. He seemed to be truly favoured.

Of course, the passage tells us that all this was in God's hands. 'The Lord was with him' and caused the things that Joseph did to be successful. He wasn't alone and he hadn't been forgotten.

It can be hard, in the midst of trouble or change, to believe that anything can be right again. Joseph's story encourages us to hold on to faith and trust that God will be with us through the turmoil. There is no situation so dire that it cannot be transformed by God's love.

Help me to trust, Lord, that you are always with me, no matter how hard it is to believe. Strengthen my faith and give me hope.

AMANDA BLOOR

Dangerous liaisons

Now Joseph was handsome and good-looking. And after a time his master's wife cast her eyes on Joseph and said, 'Lie with me.' But he refused and said to his master's wife, 'Look, with me here, my master has no concern about anything in the house, and he has put everything that he has in my hand. He is not greater in this house than I am… How then could I do this great wickedness, and sin against God?'

Just when it seemed that everything was going well, Joseph's life became complicated again. He had risen from slavery to hold a trusted position; but with influence came visibility. It is possible that Potiphar, who left the running of his household in Joseph's hands and had concern only for 'the food that he ate', had become a pampered, overweight official rather than the physically fit soldier he must have once been. Certainly, the young Israelite, 'handsome and good-looking' (v. 6), caught the eye of his master's wife, who attempted to seduce him.

Joseph, still young and naive in the ways of the world, turned aside her advances with less tact than a more experienced man might have employed. His describing an affair as 'great wickedness' (v. 9) and explaining that he could not betray the trust that Potiphar had placed in him merely encouraged her ardour. Pursuing Joseph with determination, Potiphar's wife refused to accept his rejection of her advances until she became angered by the former slave's intransigence and determined to seek revenge. A false accusation of attempted rape saw Joseph once more in trouble and committed to prison.

Our relationships with others can be a source of delight and support, but in some cases misunderstandings can cause much harm. It's hard to envisage what Joseph could have done to retrieve the situation; he knew that he had to act with integrity, following God's laws. For him, conscience and character had priority over his own safety or reputation. What matters most to us: what we know about our actions or what others believe?

Lord Jesus, you were unfairly criticised by your enemies. Help me to withstand those who would attack me without cause, so that I may hold on to what is right.

AMANDA BLOOR

God in the darkness

But the Lord was with Joseph and showed him steadfast love; he gave him favour in the sight of the chief jailer. The chief jailer committed to Joseph's care all the prisoners who were in the prison, and whatever was done there, he was the one who did it. The chief jailer paid no heed to anything that was in Joseph's care, because the Lord was with him; and whatever he did, the Lord made it prosper.

'Steadfast love' – it's a wonderful phrase, summing up the constancy and generosity of God. The passage doesn't give us any indication about how Joseph felt about being thrown into prison, but it can't have been a comfortable situation for him. Powerless once more, dependent upon the goodwill of others, he had had no trial or chance to plead his case and must have known that his life hung in the balance despite his innocence and the loyalty he had shown to his master.

Yet God was there. Joseph's qualities were noticed by the chief jailer (how lazy many officials are shown to be in this story!), and he was given responsibility for caring for the other prisoners. The text tells us that Joseph 'waited on them' and that all that he did prospered with God's help.

Most of us will have at some time found ourselves in a place of darkness, where there seems no escape. It's easy to sink into gloom and despondency, thinking that all is hopeless and that God is very distant. Joseph's experiences should encourage us to hold on and trust. God's love is 'steadfast'; God's promises to be with us are trustworthy.

Joseph had no idea what would happen next, but he got on with what had to be done – the menial domestic tasks of caring for others – with no end in sight and no hope of rescue. It could be that the very routine of looking after the other prisoners gave him dignity, purpose and self-respect; it's harder to become introspective when busy thinking about others' needs. God was with him and he was loved.

Almighty God, when I feel alone or misunderstood, remind me that you are with me and that your love is steadfast.

AMANDA BLOOR

Prophecies and hopes

One night they both dreamed – the cupbearer and the baker of the king of Egypt, who were confined in the prison… When Joseph came to them in the morning, he saw that they were troubled. So he asked Pharaoh's officers, who were with him in custody in his master's house, 'Why are your faces downcast today?' They said to him, 'We have had dreams, and there is no one to interpret them.' And Joseph said to them, 'Do not interpretations belong to God? Please tell them to me.'

I don't know whether to be impressed or exasperated! The last time Joseph interpreted dreams for his brothers and his parents, things went badly. He was accused of pride and sowed the seeds of resentment that led to his enslavement in Egypt. Yet as soon as he heard that his fellow prisoners had had troublesome dreams that they believed to be prophetic, he offered to interpret them, without a moment's thought for the possible consequences.

The first dream was given a positive interpretation: the chief cupbearer would be pardoned by Pharaoh. The chief baker, however, was told that he was to be hanged. Joseph gave the news to both prisoners almost dispassionately. It is clear that he was acting in the certainty that God had given him the gift of interpretation and that God's gifts had to be used. Good news or bad, a genuine prophet must speak truth without fear or favour.

Joseph had hoped that Pharaoh's cupbearer, once restored to his old position, would work to set him free. The cupbearer, however, went back to his duties and forgot the cellmate who had prophesied the ruler's favour upon him. It was not until Pharaoh himself began to dream, two whole years later, that Joseph had the opportunity to use his gifts again. Until that point, he had to remain faithful and trust that in God's own time he would gain his liberty.

Gracious God, I know that there are times when I am afraid to speak of what I know to be true, to stand up for what I believe to be right or to do what I know to be necessary. Give me courage to keep trying, even if I have failed before.

AMANDA BLOOR

Speaking truth to power

Pharaoh said to Joseph, 'I have had a dream, and there is no one who can interpret it…' Joseph answered Pharaoh, 'It is not I; God will give Pharaoh a favourable answer'… Then Joseph said to Pharaoh, 'Pharaoh's dreams are one and the same; God has revealed to Pharaoh what he is about to do… And the doubling of Pharaoh's dream means that the thing is fixed by God, and God will shortly bring it about.'

Pharaoh was troubled by vivid dreams and anxious to find out their meanings. Turning first to his magicians, he was pointed towards Joseph by his chief cupbearer, guiltily aware of the promise he had made to help free the young Israelite. Once more, Joseph spoke straightforwardly, without fear or reservation. Many people in his position might have tried to manipulate the situation to gain credit in the hope of regaining freedom, but Joseph was scrupulous in declaring that any facility in inter-pretation came not from his own skills, but from God. 'It is not I, but God who does this,' he declared.

An absolute ruler, Pharaoh would have been used to the flattery and political manoeuvring of court officials. He might have found Joseph's directness refreshing, or perhaps he recognised both truth and common sense in the words spoken to him. He not only set the young man free, but he also gave him responsibility in overseeing the gathering in of food against the famine to come. With one command, Joseph's life was trans-formed. For the next seven years he had authority over the whole of Egypt.

It can be daunting to speak truth to power, and history is filled with stories of saints and martyrs who have discovered that honesty is not always popular. But we are called in our lives to follow Christ's example, wherever that may lead us. Are we able to stand up for what we believe to be good and true, no matter how that is received by others?

Lord, you refused to be cowed by threats or seduced by flattery. Give me the courage to do and say what is right, especially when it is difficult to do so.

AMANDA BLOOR

God sent me here

Then Joseph said to his brothers, 'Come closer to me.' And they came closer. He said, 'I am your brother Joseph, whom you sold into Egypt. And now do not be distressed, or angry with yourselves, because you sold me here; for God sent me before you to preserve life… God sent me before you to preserve for you a remnant on earth, and to keep alive for you many survivors. So it was not you who sent me here, but God.'

At last all of the threads have been untangled. Joseph, having gathered all his brothers together, was convinced that they had learned maturity and selflessness. When Simeon was held hostage against their return, the others interpreted this as a deserved punishment from God for their violence towards Joseph. When Reuben persuaded Jacob to let Benjamin go with them as they travelled to Egypt for a second time, he offered his own sons as surety that they would keep the boy safe. And when Joseph threatened to imprison Benjamin, it was Judah, the brother responsible for selling Joseph into slavery, who pleaded to take the youngster's place.

Joseph had tested them all and was satisfied. Sending all his servants away, he called forward his brothers, embraced them and wept. With no sense at all of superiority or desire for vengeance, he generously interpreted all that had happened as being part of God's greater plan; through his journey into Egypt, 'a remnant' of Israel had been saved from famine, and many had survived what had looked like certain death. The brothers' evil intentions had been used, by God, for good.

How many of us, I wonder, are able to see God's hand in our troubles? I find it difficult to think that a loving God would willingly inflict sorrow on any of us, but I believe that if we hand over our lives – even at their worst – they can be transformed. 'It was not you who sent me here, but God,' said Joseph to his brothers (v. 8). And God is good.

Be gentle with me, God, when things go wrong. Transform my life that it may be used always for good.

AMANDA BLOOR

Endings and beginnings

When the report was heard in Pharaoh's house, 'Joseph's brothers have come', Pharaoh and his servants were pleased. Pharaoh said to Joseph, 'Say to your brothers, "Do this: load your animals and go back to the land of Canaan. Take your father and your households and come to me, so that I may give you the best of the land of Egypt, and you may enjoy the fat of the land."'

As one story draws to a close, another begins. Pharaoh, who respected Joseph's skills in administration as well as prophecy, was happy to welcome his extended family, servants and livestock into the kingdom of Egypt. They found shelter there from the famine that ravaged the land and relief from the relentless effort of carving out a living as farmers. Joseph's wealth and position ensured that they were given employment with Pharaoh and good country in which to settle; they increased in financial security and grew in numbers.

For Jacob, Joseph's father, it was a bittersweet moment. He had not only been reunited with the son he believed to be dead, but he had also met and blessed the grandsons he had not known to exist. Yet Egypt was not where he belonged; neither was it the land that God had promised would pass from Abraham and Isaac to him and his offspring. He longed to return to his homeland and on his deathbed made Joseph promise to return his bones to the cave in which his ancestors lay.

Joseph's story reminds us that human power and influence are transient. The favour of his father led to the hatred of his brothers. Position in Potiphar's household meant little against the vengeance of Potiphar's wife. And, although Joseph's family were safe while Pharaoh lived and Joseph's authority in Egypt was maintained, in the future they would be seen as a threat. Slavery and misery lay ahead for the people of Israel, and only God would be able to set them free.

All-powerful God, put far from me the desire for wealth or power. Help me to remember that all I have is your gift and bless me with the knowledge that in you, I have all that I need.

AMANDA BLOOR

Psalms 1—14

Many people feel that January is a cold month with not much to look forward to, as the sometimes shocking credit-card bills from the Christmas season arrive and the weather in the northern hemisphere hangs stark and damp. Often a sense of lament is in the air. Thus, the end of January can be a good time to delve into the opening psalms, for the first 14 mainly express lament, with a few punctuations of praise.

The psalter is the Bible's songbook, and we can't accuse it of glossing over the wrenching situations we may face in a fallen world. Betrayal, accusation, hurt – the psalmist offers the pain and heartbreak back to God, asking him to sort it out. These songs are uttered in desperation and despair, when the psalmist feels oppressed, mocked, hurting. And although the individual psalms may be filled with lament, they often end in a stanza of praise. The one voicing their feelings has reached a resolution as they express their trust and confidence in God.

Mainly these psalms are 'of David', meaning that he was probably the author but they could have been attributed to him by some who followed him. Although the songs address specific situations, David phrases them in general terms, so that they can be prayed by the Israelites at other times – and by us too.

The Psalms may be our only source of prayers at times. This is what someone close to me found when he experienced many difficulties, along with anxiety and fear. For a season, he could only read the Psalms. He says that they were enough to feed him gently during that tender time. He could express his pain and sorrow along with the hope of affirming the exclamations of praise and faith. These songs from centuries past acted as a lifeline in that dark time.

Whether we feel as if we're travelling in a cloudy tunnel or we're experiencing the joy of sunshine and warmth, the Psalms can accompany our journey with God, helping us to root our emotions in his promises.

I've been helped with these notes by several commentaries, including *Psalms* by Tremper Longman III (IVP, 2014) and *Psalms*, volume one in the NIV Application Commentary series by Gerald H. Wilson (Zondervan, 2002).

AMY BOUCHER PYE

Warning!

Blessed is the one who does not walk in step with the wicked or stand in the way that sinners take or sit in the company of mockers, but whose delight is in the law of the Lord, and who meditates on his law day and night. That person is like a tree planted by streams of water, which yields its fruit in season and whose leaf does not wither – whatever they do prospers. Not so the wicked! They are like chaff that the wind blows away.

'Look away now…' When I first moved to Britain, I was unfamiliar with the practice of newsreaders who would protect the enjoyment of sports fans by warning them of the match results soon appearing on the screen. I wondered how many fans would indeed look away, and how many would give in to the desire to know if their team had won or lost.

Psalm 1 acts as an ancient 'look away now', for it names in a few words the choices and consequences of living in God's world. One biblical commentator likens this psalm to a gateway to a literary sanctuary; that is, he sees it telling people not to read further in the Psalms if they will not obey and delight in God's law. Psalm 1 acts as an introduction to the whole psalter, and it wasn't even numbered until perhaps the end of the first century.

The choices are stark: those who 'delight in the law of the Lord' (v. 2) are blessed, but not so the wicked, who are as weightless as chaff (v. 4). Note the grammar of the blessed having been 'planted by streams of water' (v. 3), which with its passive tense refers to the hand of God the planter, who causes the fruit to grow.

As we read on in the Psalms, may we choose the way of the blessed as we delight in God's word.

Creator God, you formed the heavens and the earth and you have given me life. Through your Holy Spirit, help me to meditate on your word, chewing it over that I might follow you. Let all that is within me bless your holy name.

AMY BOUCHER PYE

Our ruler God

Why do the nations conspire and the peoples plot in vain? The kings of the earth rise up and the rulers band together against the Lord and against his anointed, saying, 'Let us break their chains and throw off their shackles'… He rebukes them in his anger and terrifies them in his wrath, saying, 'I have installed my king on Zion, my holy mountain.' I will proclaim the Lord's decree: He said to me, 'You are my son; today I have become your father.'

Psalm 2 continues the overall introduction of the psalter as it shows on a national level what happens when leaders reject God. Although these rulers band against the Lord, he rebukes them, revealing himself as the most powerful. For against them he installs his anointed one, his representative. This psalm would have been read out during the induction of a new king in David's line – although most of these monarchs failed to live up to God's standards.

Psalm 2 has a messianic meaning as well. When Jesus was baptised, the Father said, 'This is my Son, whom I love; with him I am well pleased' (Matthew 3:17), which echoes Psalm 2:7. And Peter and John quote Psalm 2 after being thrown in jail by the Sanhedrin, having shared their testimony about Jesus and his saving work on the cross (see Acts 4:23–26). Upon their release, they prayed, affirming that although Herod and Pontius Pilate conspired against Jesus, they knew God had ordained it; they sought God's help to continue to speak his word with boldness (Acts 4:27–29).

Today we may despair at the political situations in various countries around the world and at those who pursue their own interests at the cost of others and the environment. We can, and should, be involved in politics, however we interpret the various needs and issues (and Christians will often differ in their interpretations). But we shouldn't forget to pray, acknowledging that God is the overall ruler and leader, who one day will fully usher in a new kingdom of peace and joy. We can work with him in our limited capacities to welcome that kingdom now, here on this broken earth.

What could you do today to pursue God's reign on earth?

AMY BOUCHER PYE

Peaceful sleep

Lord, how many are my foes! How many rise up against me! Many are saying of me, 'God will not deliver him.' But you, Lord, are a shield around me, my glory, the One who lifts my head high. I call out to the Lord, and he answers me from his holy mountain. I lie down and sleep; I wake again, because the Lord sustains me. I will not fear though tens of thousands assail me on every side... From the Lord comes deliverance. May your blessing be on your people.

For modern people, sleep can prove elusive. When someone asks us how we are, a common answer is, 'Tired.' Parents of new babies long for a night of unbroken sleep, as delighted as they are to have a new addition in their lives. Women in midlife can suffer hormonal changes that keep them awake. Stress, screens and being overly committed can keep us from deep sleep. But as we see in Psalm 3, God can provide us rest. Although David was on the run from his plotting son, he expresses such confidence in God that he's able to sleep peacefully.

Psalm 3 is the first of the 150 that doesn't introduce the others, and the first that lists a title and author. Although David wrote the song for a specific moment in time, he also wrote it in a general manner so that it could be prayed by people throughout the ages. Note the confidence that David expresses; he says that God is a shield 'around' him (v. 3) – he feels safe not only from the dangers in front of him, but from those on the side and behind as well. And God is the one who lifts his head, not in pride but in confidence.

Tonight, before you go to sleep, why not run through the day, expressing thanks to God for the way he guided and led you? Ask him to sustain you through the night, that you might wake up refreshed and rejoicing.

Lord, you have created me with limits and needs. Help me not to ignore my body, but to care for it, that I might praise you with joy.

AMY BOUCHER PYE

Trusting God in the dark

Answer me when I call to you, my righteous God. Give me relief from my distress; have mercy on me and hear my prayer. How long will you people turn my glory into shame? How long will you love delusions and seek false gods? Know that the Lord has set apart his faithful servant for himself; the Lord hears when I call to him. Tremble and do not sin; when you are on your beds, search your hearts and be silent. Offer the sacrifices of the righteous and trust in the Lord.

When we experience difficulty, we might feel as if our prayers are going unanswered, with God far away from us. This sense of separation from God then intensifies our loneliness and can lead us to despair. We might call our experience a 'dark night of the soul', after St John of the Cross, but actually his poem 'Dark Night', the inspiration for the phrase, spoke of something different. He outlined the movement of the soul to God, for during times of darkness our souls may undergo purification that leads to union with God.

When we feel far from God, wherever we are in our journey with him, we can cry out to the Lord as David did, asking God to answer us when we call and to give us relief from our pain (v. 1). We too can exclaim, 'How long?' (v. 2). As we join David in praying through this psalm, we educate our feelings. That is, we remind ourselves that the Lord hears us when we call to him (v. 3); we tell ourselves not to sin and to search our hearts before him (v. 4).

During times of stress and pain, we may sense God's presence, but we also might need to sit in the silence, trusting in him (v. 5). For whether or not we feel him near us, he promises to be with us. He guides us through the dark times and joins us in union with him.

Lord, come to me when I call to you, and leave me not. Help me to trust you even when I can't sense your presence. You are my God; I know you love me.

AMY BOUCHER PYE

Speaking out to God

Listen to my words, Lord, consider my lament. Hear my cry for help, my King and my God, for to you I pray. In the morning, Lord, you hear my voice; in the morning I lay my requests before you and wait expectantly... Lead me, Lord, in your righteousness because of my enemies – make your way straight before me... Declare them guilty, O God! Let their intrigues be their downfall... But let all who take refuge in you be glad; let them ever sing for joy. Spread your protection over them, that those who love your name may rejoice in you.

In the first century, monasteries were called communities of mumblers, for reading was a communal and audible activity, not something done silently or individually. The monks, meditating on scripture, would mouth the words as they went about their physical labour. One monk was likened to a buzzing bee as he murmured the Psalms. This physical act of reading may have emerged because of the limited copies of scripture available, but this activity set the text deeply into the hearts and minds of the monks.

The form of the Hebrew words in this opening passage indicates this kind of private murmuring before God; the psalmist would have whispered the words to himself as he asked God to hear his cry and sighing. Often the opening words of a psalm are for praising God, but in this case they signal lament. David utters them because his enemies seem to be triumphing and his soul is downcast. So he takes to prayer, asking God to intervene and to spread his protection over those whom he loves.

We might get some strange looks if we mumbled our prayers while going about our daily tasks, but in the privacy of our own homes, we could consider adding this ancient practice of speaking out a passage from scripture. Through voicing the words, we involve our bodies. The words can take root and, with the help of the Holy Spirit, change us.

'Let the words of my mouth and the meditation of my heart be acceptable to you, O Lord, my rock and my redeemer' (Psalm 19:14, NRSV).

AMY BOUCHER PYE

How long, Lord?

Lord, do not rebuke me in your anger or discipline me in your wrath. Have mercy on me, Lord, for I am faint; heal me, Lord, for my bones are in agony. My soul is in deep anguish. How long, Lord, how long? Turn, Lord, and deliver me; save me because of your unfailing love. Among the dead no one proclaims your name. Who praises you from his grave? I am worn out from my groaning. All night long I flood my bed with weeping and drench my couch with tears.

One day when Jesus was walking with his disciples, they saw a man who was born blind. Jesus' friends asked him, 'Who sinned, this man or his parents, that he was born blind?' Jesus must have surprised them when he answered, 'Neither.' He said that through this man, God's works would be seen (see John 9:1–3).

We can read Psalm 6 with this gospel story in mind, for we might sometimes assume that sin causes one's suffering through illness or disease. After all, the psalmist starts out with a tearful lament, asking God not to punish or rebuke him but to heal him, for his 'bones are in agony' (v. 2). Perhaps he thinks that something he's done wrong has caused his groaning and physical pain.

Our silly or sinful actions *can* at times cause us physical suffering, such as if we drive while intoxicated and crash the car. But many people experience chronic illness or disease simply because we live in a world that is not as God created it to be. Since Adam and Eve sinned in the garden of Eden, ushering in sin and death, life has never been the same.

But we have a caring God, who hears us when we pray, bringing us hope and comfort. We know, with David, that 'the Lord has heard my cry for mercy' (v. 9). May we continue to bring before God those whose bones ache for healing.

'"He will wipe every tear from their eyes. There will be no more death" or mourning or crying or pain, for the old order of things has passed away'
(Revelation 21:4).

AMY BOUCHER PYE

The righteous one

Lord my God, I take refuge in you; save and deliver me from all who pursue me, or they will tear me apart like a lion and rip me to pieces with no one to rescue me. Lord my God, if I have done this and there is guilt on my hands – if I have repaid my ally with evil or without cause have robbed my foe – then let my enemy pursue and overtake me; let him trample my life to the ground and make me sleep in the dust... Vindicate me, Lord, according to my righteousness, according to my integrity, O Most High. Bring to an end the violence of the wicked and make the righteous secure – you, the righteous God who probes minds and hearts.

If you'd like to explore how Jesus appears in the psalter, I warmly recommend Patrick Henry Reardon's *Christ in the Psalms* (Concilliar Press, 2000). With thoughtful prose, he cites how these ancient songs foreshadow the coming Son of God. His insights on Psalm 7 are particularly helpful, for he points to Jesus as the only one who can truly pray this song. After all, how many of us have no guilt on our hands (v. 3) or can ask God to vindicate us according to our righteousness and integrity (v. 8)? I only have to think through the previous days or week to know that I do not qualify.

Because we have union with God through Christ, Reardon says we pray this psalm properly through entering 'into the mind of the Lord in the context of His redemptive Passion'. We don't pray it to express our personal feelings, but 'to discover something of His' (p. 14).

How do you react to this idea? Part of me is intrigued, but part of me wonders if we're elevating ourselves too high in a quest to experience what Jesus felt. And yet God promises that Jesus dwells within us – an amazing mystery. I'm off to ponder some more.

'I have been crucified with Christ and I no longer live, but Christ lives in me. The life I now live in the body, I live by faith in the Son of God, who loved me and gave himself for me' (Galatians 2:20).

AMY BOUCHER PYE

Our wonderful God

Lord, our Lord, how majestic is your name in all the earth! You have set your glory in the heavens. Through the praise of children and infants you have established a stronghold against your enemies, to silence the foe and the avenger. When I consider your heavens, the work of your fingers, the moon and the stars, which you have set in place, what is mankind that you are mindful of them, human beings that you care for them? You have made them a little lower than the angels and crowned them with glory and honour... Lord, our Lord, how majestic is your name in all the earth!

A friend of mine makes sure that each day she stops and ponders something in creation as an act of worship to God. One day she may hold a stone in her hand, feeling its cold weight as she considers how God is her rock and foundation. Another day she may gaze at a leaf with its slender veins and colours of green. Another day she may watch the cloud formations gliding across the sky. As she wonders at creation, she returns thanks to God, the creator.

Reaching Psalm 8, with its burst of praise for our God who created the heavens and the earth, feels refreshing after a week of psalms of lament and pleas for deliverance. Note how the psalm begins and ends with the refrain about the majesty of the Lord's name in all the earth (vv. 1, 9). These sentences serve as bookends, rooting the song as an expression of worship and honour to God.

Although creation is magnificent, so much more is humanity, who has been created in God's image. Although we have been made 'a little lower than the angels', we've yet been crowned with God's glory and given dominion over the earth (vv. 5–6).

Why not stop and consider something from creation today, giving thanks as you examine it? Then ponder the gift of being made in God's image. What an amazing thought!

Lord, we praise you and worship you! You fill the earth with your glory; you dwell in the hearts of those who love you. Turn our faces to you, to receive your love.

AMY BOUCHER PYE

Praying for the nations

I will give thanks to you, Lord, with all my heart; I will tell of all your wonderful deeds. I will be glad and rejoice in you; I will sing the praises of your name, O Most High… But God will never forget the needy; the hope of the afflicted will never perish. Arise, Lord, do not let mortals triumph; let the nations be judged in your presence. Strike them with terror, Lord; let the nations know they are only mortal.

Biblical scholars believe that Psalms 9 and 10 originally appeared as one psalm. They aren't sure why these poems were later split into two, but the lack of a title for Psalm 10 hints to their previous form. A bigger clue, however, is the poetic nature of the psalms, for they are an acrostic poem. That means that the first letter of each line begins with a successive letter of the Hebrew alphabet. Psalm 9 covers the first half, while Psalm 10 the second.

Why does it matter that Psalm 9 and 10 used to be one? When we read them as a whole, we can see a movement from emphasising the individual to an awareness of the needs of the nations. The flow moves outwards, with the focus turning to the collective. In ancient cultures, this wouldn't have been unusual, but in western societies today the individual as the unit of concern seems to reign unchecked.

As Christians we're called to be countercultural when the ways of our societies go against God's teaching, such as the unspoken rule that people should be most concerned for themselves. We can ask God to intervene, petitioning with David that God would not forget the needy or the afflicted (v. 18). And we can affirm that 'the Lord is known by his acts of justice' (v. 16) as we pray that the nations would understand that they are only mortal (v. 20).

Expanding our prayers beyond our borders becomes an enriching exercise in learning how to love the world and its peoples.

Lord, we grieve at the acts of terror we witness today. Please help us to learn to live peacefully with each other.

AMY BOUCHER PYE

Deadly pride

In his arrogance the wicked man hunts down the weak, who are caught in the schemes he devises. He boasts about the cravings of his heart; he blesses the greedy and reviles the Lord. In his pride the wicked man does not seek him; in all his thoughts there is no room for God... He says to himself, 'Nothing will ever shake me.' He swears, 'No one will ever do me harm.' His mouth is full of lies and threats; trouble and evil are under his tongue... He says to himself, 'God will never notice; he covers his face and never sees.' Arise, Lord! Lift up your hand, O God.

Of the seven deadly sins – pride, greed, lust, envy, gluttony, wrath and sloth – pride is seen as the most pernicious and as the source of the others. Those beholden to pride think they are better than others and God, and therefore are entitled to many acquisitions (greed), able to exercise their bodily attractions freely (lust), resentful of the gifts of others (envy), gorging of their hunger (gluttony), angered over the actions of others (wrath) and not motivated to worship God (sloth).

Psalm 10 (or more accurately the second half of Psalm 9) names the deeds of the prideful person and the havoc they wreak. They are pitted against God and his work as they lie, plot, boast and assume that all that they do will prosper. But David calls on God to lift up his hand and not to forget the helpless (v. 12). For God is the king, says David, who defends 'the fatherless and the oppressed' (vv. 16, 18). David puts his hope in God, even though he sees prideful people all around him.

Although the Psalms were written so long ago, they reverberate with meaning today. No doubt you can think of prideful people, whether leaders of nations or someone in your community. We can ask God to limit their influence and to defend the cause of the oppressed. May God's rule be embraced all over the earth.

Father, you care for the downtrodden and overlooked, for the refugee and the homeless. Open my eyes to the needs of those near me and those far from me. Help me to spread your love and care.

AMY BOUCHER PYE

Learning to discern

In the Lord I take refuge. How then can you say to me: 'Flee like a bird to your mountain. For look, the wicked bend their bows; they set their arrows against the strings to shoot from the shadows at the upright in heart. When the foundations are being destroyed, what can the righteous do?' The Lord is in his holy temple; the Lord is on his heavenly throne. He observes everyone on earth; his eyes examine them... For the Lord is righteous, he loves justice; the upright will see his face.

Learning to discern the voice of God is a key part of maturing as a follower of Christ. As we hear God, we should test out our understanding through prayer and discussion with wise Christians as to whether we have indeed heard God. When we grow in this way, we'll then be able to stand against the scoffers and those telling us to ignore the ways of God.

David had a strong relationship with God and thus was able to resist those pitted against him who told him to flee like a bird in times of trouble (v. 1). These advisers, according to biblical commentators, seem to mock David with their sparse comments, which in the Hebrew contain no prepositions, implying minimum engagement with what David is saying. Instead, David looks to the source of his strength, God. As he says, the Lord might be high on his throne, but he's concerned for everyone on earth, his eyes examining them (v. 4). David knows that those who are upright before God will see his face (v. 7).

Discernment about God's ways means knowing when to stand against those opposed to us and when, in contrast, to relent. When we approach God with humility, asking him to enlighten us with wisdom, we can trust that he will help us. He might lead us to a new friendship with a wise Christian; he might quicken some biblical texts that speak to our situation; he might inspire us through his Holy Spirit. I pray we will all continue to grow in wisdom and discernment.

'If any of you lacks wisdom, you should ask God, who gives generously to all without finding fault, and it will be given to you' (James 1:5).

AMY BOUCHER PYE

Words of life, words of death

Everyone lies to their neighbour; they flatter with their lips but harbour deception in their hearts. May the Lord silence all flattering lips and every boastful tongue – those who say, 'By our tongues we will prevail; our own lips will defend us – who is lord over us?' 'Because the poor are plundered and the needy groan, I will now arise,' says the Lord. 'I will protect them from those who malign them.' And the words of the Lord are flawless, like silver purified in a crucible, like gold refined seven times.

If you've been the subject of gossip, you know how painful the experience can be. People pass on idle speculation or outright lies; those without the full story pontificate about matters about which they should remain silent. Of course, we all have probably had loose lips at times, later regretting and hopefully repenting of the words we should have kept unspoken.

David was the subject of gossip and speculation on more than one occasion. Being a leader, he was talked about for the decisions he made and those he didn't make – as are leaders today. No doubt sometimes the assessments about David were fair, and sometimes they were not.

But David recognises that the words of the Lord are flawless; they are like precious metals that have been purified and refined (v. 6). Those who follow God will learn to speak truth as the Holy Spirit dwells in them, and often as they face trials of many kinds. Through these trials they will be purified as silver and gold, as echoed by Peter in his letter: 'These have come so that the proven genuineness of your faith – of greater worth than gold, which perishes even though refined by fire – may result in praise, glory and honour when Jesus Christ is revealed' (1 Peter 1:7).

May our words reflect God's truth and bring glory to him as we build up our fellow believers and reach out with love to those who do not know God.

Lord Jesus Christ, you are the Word who was with God and was God.
As the Word you took on flesh and dwelled among us.
Fill us with your presence this day. (After John 1.)

AMY BOUCHER PYE

A song of lament

How long, Lord? Will you forget me for ever? How long will you hide your face from me? How long must I wrestle with my thoughts and day after day have sorrow in my heart? How long will my enemy triumph over me? Look on me and answer, Lord my God... But I trust in your unfailing love; my heart rejoices in your salvation. I will sing the Lord's praise, for he has been good to me.

The prayer of lament, previously overlooked by many Christians, is now becoming more popular. As we've seen, the Psalms are a repository of prayers of lament as the psalmist complains and cries out to God – even demanding his help at times. When the dysfunction, whether through accusation, persecution or sickness, reaches an unacceptable level, the psalmist voices his concerns to God.

These psalms of lament move from an articulation of hurt and anger to submission to God and then a state of relinquishment. Through prayer the psalmist is transformed, reaching a certainty about the goodness of God. He knows that the Lord has heard his prayer, and he trusts that God will act to save him.

Psalm 13 is short, but raises the persistent question four times: 'How long, Lord?' These words convey the sense that God knows that injustice is happening and isn't doing anything about it. The psalmist asks for God to remedy this matter. And then in a surprising change of voice, he expresses his trust in God, affirming that God is good and faithful (vv. 5–6).

What difference does it make to have a faith that permits and even requires this kind of prayer? One benefit is that the person praying feels heard by God. They have a voice and are allowed to speak other than only in thanksgiving and praise; they need not feel guilty expressing hurt or anger about the state of the world or their circumstances. They trust that God is big enough to handle their fears and their disappointment.

If you need to express lament, know that God welcomes your prayers.

Lord, when we hear news of ill health or a betrayal, our hearts cry out within us. Please bring healing and comfort.

AMY BOUCHER PYE

True foolishness

The fool says in his heart, 'There is no God.' They are corrupt, their deeds are vile; there is no one who does good. The Lord looks down from heaven on all mankind to see if there are any who understand, any who seek God. All have turned away, all have become corrupt; there is no one who does good, not even one... Oh, that salvation for Israel would come out of Zion! When the Lord restores his people, let Jacob rejoice and Israel be glad!

As we come to the end of exploring these opening psalms, we reach a meditation on true foolishness – those who say there is no God. David doesn't declare that fools are those who are ignorant, but rather those who choose in their heart, through pondering and deliberation, to turn from God. Perhaps David has in mind his encounter with Nabal (whose very name meant fool), the husband of Abigail who spurned giving David and his men hospitality (see 1 Samuel 25). Again, David employs general terms so that the psalm can be prayed by many people.

In the second verse, God 'looks down from heaven'. This same sense of God being ever present in his creation, watching with sadness as his people turn from him, appears elsewhere in the Old Testament, including in the story of the tower of Babel (see Genesis 11:1–9).

Moving to the end of the psalm, David turns from a wisdom meditation to a lament as he cries out to God, asking him to restore his people (v. 7). Again the voicing of the psalmist's thoughts is a vehicle for him to come to a resolution, this time through a petition.

As you think back over the past fortnight, consider how you've responded to the psalms we've explored. If you've found yourself reacting strongly to one of them, whether in feelings of consolation or desolation, take some time to consider prayerfully why that might be.

May we feel free to voice our feelings of praise and lament to the one who created us.

Lord, thank you for these songs that have been prayed for so many years. Help us to find comfort and hope in you through them.

AMY BOUCHER PYE

Sheep and shepherding in John's gospel

One of my most treasured books is *Bible Animals* by J.G. Wood (1892). It was a school prize won by my grandfather in the 1890s, full of engravings and beautifully bound. It devotes more space to sheep than to any other animal.

At the time of Jesus, raising and caring for sheep had long been a vital part of the Israelite economy. In the early days of Israel, almost every family owned a few sheep, so someone in the family was a shepherd; Moses and David are just two examples. Sheep were hardy and could live outdoors all year. They needed water every day but could live off sparse grass if necessary. The sheep were kept for milk and wool as well as meat, so we need to think of long-lived sheep rather than the pattern of breed, fatten and slaughter that we see today. The shepherd had the whole natural lifetime of the sheep to get to know them, living with the same sheep for many years.

We're often told that in Jesus' day shepherding was a despised occupation, hence the contrasts often made between the two groups who visited the baby Jesus, the magi and the shepherds. It seems that after the exile the occupation of shepherd had become devalued. Shepherds were no longer members of the family who owned the sheep, but often people working for pay.

Jesus' contemporaries may have despised shepherds, but this was the image Jesus chose to illustrate God's love for his wayward people. In predicting his death, Jesus describes himself as the good shepherd laying down his life for his sheep. His death is also explained in terms of a sacrificial lamb. Furthermore, Jesus invites us to look ahead to a time when God's shepherding of his people will be fulfilled by sheep-turned-shepherds, the followers of Jesus.

It has been suggested that language about sheep and shepherds is outmoded these days. Most people know little about contemporary farming, never mind the life of a shepherd and his sheep 2,000 years ago, so let's find new images for the 21st century. I think that view is misguided. The images of sheep and shepherd continue to help us to understand God's plan of redemption and to appreciate his great love for us.

ROSIE WARD

The Lord is my shepherd

The Lord is my shepherd, I shall not want. He makes me lie down in green pastures; he leads me beside still waters; he restores my soul. He leads me in right paths for his name's sake. Even though I walk through the darkest valley, I fear no evil; for you are with me; your rod and your staff – they comfort me. You prepare a table before me in the presence of my enemies; you anoint my head with oil; my cup overflows. Surely goodness and mercy shall follow me all the days of my life, and I shall dwell in the house of the Lord my whole life long.

For many years a toy sheep has taken pride of place on my chest of drawers. It was given to me by members of a group I led, who presented it to their 'shepherdess'. It reminds me of those lovely people, but also that I am primarily a sheep and that the Lord is my shepherd.

This psalm, written many years before the gospels, sets the scene for all that is to follow; it highlights the shepherd language that had been used for the leaders of God's people since the exodus. The Lord is described as 'my shepherd', and the psalm describes the day's work of a shepherd of the ancient Near East. Sheep need to be led to green pastures; in a dry land they need water. But the words conjure up so much more than satisfying basic needs. The sheep need to be kept safe: on difficult terrain the shepherd leads the way and, if necessary, uses the rod and staff to beat off wild animals or rescue a sheep that has become stuck.

This psalm invites us to a relationship of intimacy and grace. Knowing that the Lord is our shepherd, we are safe in his care. Even in the darkest valley, we need not fear if he is there to protect us. He is the *good* shepherd, and one day we will see him as the *great* shepherd, leading us to 'springs of the water of life' (Revelation 7:17).

Lord, guide me today, and keep me in your loving care. Amen.

ROSIE WARD

The lamb of God

The next day [John] saw Jesus coming towards him and declared, 'Here is the Lamb of God who takes away the sin of the world! This is he of whom I said, "After me comes a man who ranks ahead of me because he was before me"'… The next day John again was standing with two of his disciples, and as he watched Jesus walk by, he exclaimed, 'Look, here is the Lamb of God!' The two disciples heard him say this, and they followed Jesus.

A striking painting at an exhibition called 'Seeing Salvation' caught my eye. The painting is *The Bound Lamb* by Zurbarán. A young lamb with horns is lying on a stone slab, its feet bound with rope. The white lamb is set against a plain dark background.

The Old Testament offerings of an unblemished lamb, perfect, spotless, emphasising the holiness of God, came to be seen as foreshadowing the death of Christ. Isaiah speaks of a suffering servant, 'like a lamb that is led to the slaughter' (Isaiah 53:7), and the apostle Philip interprets this passage as referring to Jesus (Acts 8:32–35).

Jesus is not just *like* a lamb; he is the 'Lamb of God' (v. 36). Just as the death of the Passover lamb enabled the people of Israel to be spared the angel of death (Exodus 12:23), so this lamb will save the 'world' from judgement on sin. Sacrificial offerings could not take away sin, but God himself provided an offering, his only Son. According to John (19:14), it was the day of preparation for Passover, the day when lambs were being killed in the temple, that Jesus was nailed to the cross.

'Look,' said John the Baptist. He directed the gaze of those who listened to look more closely at Jesus. The simple words 'here is the Lamb of God' were apparently enough to prompt the first of many disciples to start following Jesus.

Who is Jesus? He is the Lamb of God who takes away the sin of the world.

'All we like sheep have gone astray; we have all turned to our own way, and the Lord has laid on him the iniquity of us all' (Isaiah 53:6).

ROSIE WARD

Zeal for God's house

The Passover of the Jews was near, and Jesus went up to Jerusalem. In the temple he found people selling cattle, sheep, and doves, and the money-changers seated at their tables. Making a whip of cords, he drove all of them out of the temple, both the sheep and the cattle. He also poured out the coins of the money-changers and overturned their tables. He told those who were selling the doves, 'Take these things out of here! Stop making my Father's house a market-place!' His disciples remembered that it was written, 'Zeal for your house will consume me.'

Imagine someone walking into the chamber of government, overturning the tables in the middle, throwing all the papers on to the floor and shouting, 'Stop all this! Stop it at once!' It's an astonishing scene! The temple was the beating heart of Jerusalem, the place where God had promised to live with his people. It was the focal point of the nation. So imagine how it must have been when an unknown prophet from Galilee entered one day and turned everything upside down.

What do we make of it? This is a somewhat different Jesus than the 'meek and mild' one we may have grown up with. Jesus brandishes a whip, gets angry. Selling animals and changing coins were necessary for the functioning of the temple, but their presence there, in the place set aside as God's dwelling, had turned it into a marketplace.

It was common for God's people to journey to the temple to get ready for this most important of festivals, the Passover. At the festival each family consumed a lamb that was without blemish, a male a year old, in memory of the exodus from Egypt (Exodus 12:5). People were celebrating that freedom from slavery and praying that God would do it again, only on a grander scale. It is at this time that Jesus visits Jerusalem, for the first time in his ministry, and walks among the sheep ready for slaughter. It's a big hint of what is to come. In the person of Jesus, Israel's God has now at last come to rescue his people.

Reflect on what the death of Jesus means to you.

ROSIE WARD

You are my sheep

For thus says the Lord God: I myself will search for my sheep, and will seek them out. As shepherds seek out their flocks when they are among their scattered sheep, so I will seek out my sheep. I will rescue them from all the places to which they have been scattered on a day of clouds and thick darkness. I will bring them out from the peoples and gather them from the countries, and will bring them into their own land... I will feed them with good pasture, and the mountain heights of Israel shall be their pasture; there they shall lie down in good grazing land, and they shall feed on rich pasture on the mountains of Israel. I myself will be the shepherd of my sheep, and I will make them lie down, says the Lord God. I will seek the lost, and I will bring back the strayed, and I will bind up the injured, and I will strengthen the weak.

By the time of Ezekiel, as nations struggled for power and Judah fell to Babylon in 598BC, shepherding was a well-established metaphor for governing. In the verses immediately before those above, Ezekiel addresses the 'shepherds' of Israel, the kings who had been ruling, accusing them of self-interest and dereliction of duty. They don't care for the weak and the sick, the straying and lost sheep. And because sheep without a shepherd are in big trouble, the sheep are scattered – in exile.

Then Ezekiel sees a time when God himself will go in search of his scattered sheep. He will find them, gather them together and bring them back to their own land, where they can graze on good pastures in security. This is the context for Jesus' use of the imagery of straying sheep (Luke 15) and the crowds being 'like sheep without a shepherd' (Matthew 9:36). Ezekiel further tells of a time when God will 'set up over them one shepherd, my servant David, and he shall feed them' (34:23), and towards the end of chapter 34 sees a time when peace and justice are finally restored to his people.

'You are my sheep, the sheep of my pasture, and I am your God, says the Lord God' (Ezekiel 34:31).

ROSIE WARD

The shepherd of the sheep

'Very truly, I tell you, anyone who does not enter the sheepfold by the gate but climbs in by another way is a thief and a bandit. The one who enters by the gate is the shepherd of the sheep. The gatekeeper opens the gate for him, and the sheep hear his voice. He calls his own sheep by name and leads them out. When he has brought out all his own, he goes ahead of them, and the sheep follow him because they know his voice.'

The sheep kept by Jesus' contemporaries were able to live outside all year, but were kept in a simple pen at night for protection. Jesus' hearers knew the demands and dangers of the shepherd's life. Struggles with wild animals, guarding the entrance, beating off intruders and many other acts of courage were necessary to keep the flock safe. A good shepherd would be willing to risk his life for the sheep, sometimes lying across the entrance to keep the sheep safe.

This sheepfold, perhaps containing several different flocks, has a gate. Picture a gatekeeper guarding the gate overnight. In the morning, the shepherd arrives and leads his sheep out to find good pasture for the day. The sheep don't recognise the voice of a stranger, but this shepherd knows his flock well, and they in turn recognise the voice of their own shepherd.

Jesus' hearers also knew that the word 'shepherd' was used to describe the nation's leaders. They were tired of those who had betrayed the idea of shepherds by caring for themselves rather than for the welfare of the people. In the preceding verses, Jesus has accused the religious leaders of being blind. 'Thieves and bandits,' he says. 'Let those who hear, understand!' Others claimed to be shepherds; he was the *good* shepherd.

And Jesus is not only the shepherd; he is also the gate, the way into the sheepfold. That is a big claim to make – that he is the fulfilment of the law and the replacement of Moses, who wrote it. That he, not the temple, is the way to God. No wonder his words were soon dividing those who heard them.

Good shepherd, thank you that I belong to you.

ROSIE WARD

How to hear God

'The gatekeeper opens the gate for him, and the sheep hear his voice. He calls his own sheep by name and leads them out. When he has brought out all his own, he goes ahead of them, and the sheep follow him because they know his voice. They will not follow a stranger, but they will run from him because they do not know the voice of strangers.' Jesus used this figure of speech with them, but they did not understand what he was saying to them.

Two children once came to my door asking if I could teach them a song we'd sung at their after-school club. It was a lively song about sheep, and how the sheep had a good shepherd looking after them. As I taught them, I prayed that they would one day know that shepherd for themselves.

Life works best when we understand that God is the good shepherd and we are his sheep. A sheep does not have to worry, because the shepherd takes care of everything: finding water and good pasture and protecting the sheep from predators.

There are just a few things that the sheep need to do. The sheep need to listen, to hear the shepherd's voice. It can be difficult to find time to sit down and listen to God – but then that's what these notes are all about: helping us to hear God. If we read and then listen prayerfully, we make space for God to speak.

I always find it amazing that in the middle of a crowd I can pick out a familiar voice – the voice of my husband or a friend. Hearing the same voice many times enables us to hear it above all the others, just as sheep that hear the voice of their shepherd many times can pick it out. As we get into the habit of listening, we get to recognise God's voice, to distinguish it from other, distracting, voices. At times, life can seem complicated and confusing. But if we take each day at a time, asking him for instruction, advice and encouragement, then we can trust that he will protect us and we will be ready to listen to his voice.

Lord, help me to listen and to follow.

ROSIE WARD

Life abundantly

So again Jesus said to them, 'Very truly, I tell you, I am the gate for the sheep. All who came before me are thieves and bandits; but the sheep did not listen to them. I am the gate. Whoever enters by me will be saved, and will come in and go out and find pasture. The thief comes only to steal and kill and destroy. I came that they may have life, and have it abundantly.'

'I came that they may have life', says Jesus. 'The thief comes only to steal and kill and destroy.' Jesus is contrasting himself with the 'thieves and bandits' – religious leaders or would-be messiah figures, who might try to enter the sheepfold and claim the sheep. In Jesus' day, when wealth was counted in cattle and sheep rather than coins and notes, there were plenty of people out to steal a few sheep.

Today, sheep rustlers come in a different guise. There are many different voices out to steal our peace of mind, to offer us quick substitutes for 'life'. Jesus is different. He is faithful, true and dependable. He is not just the way to God, the gate; he *is* God, and he gives us the life of God.

Life in abundance does not mean riches, success or the things that our society often counts as good things. The life that Jesus gives is about peace, contentment, fulfilment, joy and a love that can satisfy the deepest hunger and deepest thirst. We can be remarkably blessed and live life abundantly in the midst of difficult circumstances. Poverty and persecution cannot take away the peace that God provides for us in Christ. Life in abundance means being reconciled with God through Jesus and knowing that we are stewards of the blessings of God.

Perhaps the way to know we have an abundant life is when we have shared that life with others. When we realise that Jesus has given us life in order for us to be fully functioning, fully image-bearing human beings within God's world, we truly have life in abundance.

What does it mean to you to have life in abundance?

ROSIE WARD

Facing the wolf

'I am the good shepherd. The good shepherd lays down his life for the sheep. The hired hand, who is not the shepherd and does not own the sheep, sees the wolf coming and leaves the sheep and runs away – and the wolf snatches them and scatters them. The hired hand runs away because a hired hand does not care for the sheep. I am the good shepherd. I know my own and my own know me, just as the Father knows me and I know the Father. And I lay down my life for the sheep.'

One of my favourite children's stories is 'Montmorency the lamb'. The story revolves around Montmorency's adventures and the fact that things go wrong 'unless of course you've got a good shepherd'. Montmorency and his friends enjoy daisy soup and buttercup sandwiches, count people to get to sleep and get the wool pulled over their eyes. But one day Montmorency discovers a wolf is at the door. Luckily, Someone is lying across the entrance to the fold, blocking the door. The Someone tells Montmorency, 'You're absolutely safe. The big, bad wolf... can only get you over my dead body. And, you see, he can never get over my dead body' (quoted in Lance Pierson, *Know How to Give a Five-Minute Talk*, 1984).

Today's passage contains a simple contrast: good shepherd and hired hand. The shepherd knows the sheep by name. Someone brought in to help, the 'hired hand', is just doing it for the money. He does not know the sheep, and they don't know him. When danger comes, the hired hand is more worried about his own safety than about the sheep. He runs away. The good shepherd not only protects his sheep, but he is even willing to lay down his life for them.

We don't face many wolves in our daily lives, but there are plenty of things that make us anxious and afraid. We can feel safe knowing that there's someone who knows us by name and who is looking after us. And because he made the ultimate sacrifice – he died and he rose again – we know that we are safe with him eternally as well.

What is making you anxious or afraid at the moment?
Give those things to the good shepherd.

ROSIE WARD

One flock

'I have other sheep that do not belong to this fold. I must bring them also, and they will listen to my voice. So there will be one flock, one shepherd. For this reason the Father loves me, because I lay down my life in order to take it up again. No one takes it from me, but I lay it down of my own accord. I have power to lay it down, and I have power to take it up again. I have received this command from my Father.'

From shepherds to flocks. The shepherd cares for not just one group of sheep but several. They all listen to his voice – they know him and trust him.

As the shepherd stands for Jesus, so the flock stands for his people. Looking ahead to what will happen after his death and resurrection, Jesus sees a time when his flock will contain both sheep from 'this fold' – believers among God's people – along with others from among the Gentiles who will join them. All will become one flock under one shepherd.

It's easy to be absorbed in our own 'fold' and to forget that the church is wider than our own local expression of it. It was a challenging idea for the religious leaders at that time that Jews and non-Jews might be included in the same religious group. But it's easy for us to make the same mistake, as we continue to struggle with the question of who is 'in' and who is 'out'. The Christian world is diverse, with many different versions, and we all have our own ideas of who we want to be in the same fold as us. Here we are reminded that other sheep also belong to Jesus.

Have you ever watched a shepherd separating sheep? It's not easy! Sheep expecting two lambs may be separated from those expecting three or just one, and the shepherd deftly opens and closes a gate to separate one flock into two groups. Putting them all together is a whole lot easier – open the gate and off they go! How might we work more closely with Christians from other traditions, to demonstrate that there really is only one flock, with one shepherd?

Lord, make your people one.

ROSIE WARD

Hearing and believing

At that time the festival of the Dedication took place in Jerusalem. It was winter, and Jesus was walking in the temple, in the portico of Solomon. So the Jews gathered around him and said to him, 'How long will you keep us in suspense? If you are the Messiah, tell us plainly.' Jesus answered, 'I have told you, and you do not believe. The works that I do in my Father's name testify to me; but you do not believe, because you do not belong to my sheep. My sheep hear my voice. I know them, and they follow me.'

It was winter in Jerusalem. Out on the nearby hills shepherds huddled together with their sheep to keep warm, searching in the bitter weather for pasture to keep the sheep fed. The sheep needed to produce wool and lambs for food, clothing and sale for sacrifice. The festival of Dedication, or Hanukkah, commemorated the cleansing of the temple by Judas Maccabeus two centuries earlier. The Maccabees had briefly freed the temple from foreign domination, and as God's people looked back, so they also looked forward. When would the promised Messiah come to rescue them again?

Hence the question to Jesus. But Jesus rounds on the questioners. They are not really interested in the truth, because they are not his sheep. The sheep listen to his voice. If they don't listen, they can't be his sheep. Jesus makes it clear that whoever these leaders are, they are not up to the job of shepherding Israel. They are just like those who came before – the 'shepherds' whom the prophet Ezekiel had denounced, leaders who had failed in their duties. And those who had occupied various places of authority for the last few decades were no better.

'I have told you,' says Jesus, and they have seen his works. But it's as if they have been both blind and deaf. When it comes to recognising who Jesus is, it seems that either you get it or you don't get it. If you have faith, you will hear the shepherd's voice. Without it, you'll just be another sheep lost in the desert, desperately seeking the sparse winter pasture.

Pray for those you know who seem closed to Jesus,
that their eyes may be opened.

ROSIE WARD

Safe for eternity

Jesus answered, 'I have told you, and you do not believe. The works that I do in my Father's name testify to me; but you do not believe, because you do not belong to my sheep. My sheep hear my voice. I know them, and they follow me. I give them eternal life, and they will never perish. No one will snatch them out of my hand. What my Father has given me is greater than all else, and no one can snatch it out of the Father's hand. The Father and I are one.' The Jews took up stones again to stone him.

As I write this, it's lambing time, and lambs are playing in the fields. It's less fun for the shepherds, up all night to watch out for difficult births and to ensure that all the sheep are safe. There are diseases to watch out for, sheep rustlers and predators to guard against, and a livelihood and heritage to protect.

'I know them,' says Jesus, 'and they follow me' (v. 27). It is reassuring to know that we have such a dedicated shepherd, a personal friend and guide alongside us, especially through the dark times of our lives. We can trust that though the way may be difficult, we are safe in his hands. We can feel secure. We are also fully protected. We can't be driven out of his hands by others. No one can snatch us out of his hand – which is the Father's hand.

Whatever time of year we are reading this passage, it reminds us of the message of Easter. At the time of the Passover festival, Jesus the sacrificial lamb achieved an even greater Passover, bringing his flock over from death to life. Only Jesus cares for sheep so much that he will do anything for them, even willingly lay down his life. And the power that brought Jesus to life from death is the same power of God working for us.

'Thine be the glory, risen, conquering Son, endless is the victory thou o'er death hast won' (Edmond Louis Budry, 1854–1932).

ROSIE WARD

A new start

Jesus said to them, 'Come and have breakfast.' Now none of the disciples dared to ask him, 'Who are you?' because they knew it was the Lord. Jesus came and took the bread and gave it to them, and did the same with the fish. This was now the third time that Jesus appeared to the disciples after he was raised from the dead. When they had finished breakfast, Jesus said to Simon Peter, 'Simon son of John, do you love me more than these?' He said to him, 'Yes, Lord; you know that I love you.' Jesus said to him, 'Feed my lambs.' A second time he said to him, 'Simon son of John, do you love me?' He said to him, 'Yes, Lord; you know that I love you.' Jesus said to him, 'Tend my sheep.' He said to him the third time, 'Simon son of John, do you love me?' Peter felt hurt because he said to him the third time, 'Do you love me?' And he said to him, 'Lord, you know everything; you know that I love you.' Jesus said to him, 'Feed my sheep'.

This is probably the first close encounter Peter has had with Jesus since that fateful night in the firelit courtyard (John 18:15–18, 25–27). In his distress Peter has gone back to what he knew best, fishing. But just as he has found he can no longer do even that, there appears a stranger – albeit one strangely familiar – on the shore.

Coming after a night of fruitless fishing, there are echoes of that earlier encounter at Galilee when Jesus first commissioned Peter, when Peter acknowledged his sin in the sight of Jesus' goodness: 'I am a sinful man' (Luke 5:8). Now, after Peter has sinned once more by denying Jesus, he is standing by another flickering fire. There were three denials; now, there are three affirmations: 'Yes, Lord, you know that I love you.' Jesus' response to each one is, 'Feed my lambs... Tend my sheep... Feed my sheep'.

With each question, the painful past is confronted – and finally healed. It's his past that makes Peter who he is; now it becomes the foundation for a new future. Peter is not only forgiven; he is also recommissioned.

Think about anything in your past that troubles you.
Give it to Jesus and let him transform it.

ROSIE WARD

Do you love me?

When they had finished breakfast, Jesus said to Simon Peter, 'Simon son of John, do you love me more than these?' He said to him, 'Yes, Lord; you know that I love you.' Jesus said to him, 'Feed my lambs… Very truly, I tell you, when you were younger, you used to fasten your own belt and to go wherever you wished. But when you grow old, you will stretch out your hands, and someone else will fasten a belt around you and take you where you do not wish to go.' (He said this to indicate the kind of death by which he would glorify God.) After this he said to him, 'Follow me.'

As he prepares to leave his disciples for the last time, Jesus the good shepherd will soon no longer be able to shepherd his sheep himself. He will need under-shepherds to carry on the work. All through his ministry he has prepared his followers for this moment, and now they hear these words: 'Tend my sheep… feed my lambs.'

But before he can entrust his ministry to Peter – or to any other Christian – he needs to make sure that Peter is up to it. 'Do you love me more than these?' It's not clear whether the question is about Peter's loving Jesus more than the trappings of power, wealth or position, or whether it means, 'Do you love me more than the other disciples do?' In the end, it does not matter. Ultimately he's asking if we put Jesus first.

With a call comes a cost. John adds a note to explain that Jesus is referring to Peter's death. By the time this gospel was written, Peter had glorified God by his martyrdom, probably in Rome. Today, all over the world, Christians are suffering for their faith, and some are suffering the ultimate price. When I read about what Christians in many other countries have to face, I wonder how I would fare. 'Follow me' is an invitation to every Christian leader, every disciple, to keep following Jesus wherever that may lead.

Pray for grace to stand strong as a follower of Jesus.

ROSIE WARD

Freed to worship

They sing a new song: 'You are worthy to take the scroll and to open its seals, for you were slaughtered and by your blood you ransomed for God saints from every tribe and language and people and nation; you have made them to be a kingdom and priests serving our God, and they will reign on earth.' Then I looked, and I heard the voice of many angels surrounding the throne and the living creatures and the elders; they numbered myriads of myriads and thousands of thousands, singing with full voice, 'Worthy is the Lamb that was slaughtered to receive power and wealth and wisdom and might and honour and glory and blessing!' Then I heard every creature in heaven and on earth and under the earth and in the sea, and all that is in them, singing, 'To the one seated on the throne and to the Lamb be blessing and honour and glory and might for ever and ever!' And the four living creatures said, 'Amen!' And the elders fell down and worshipped.

We come to the climax of the Bible's big picture and of our sheep and shepherding theme. Here, in the final book of the Bible, the glimpse of God's purposes for his flock seen in the book of Ezekiel comes to its fruition. The lamb led to the slaughter, the ultimate Passover sacrifice, is now the Lamb in the throne room, surrounded by four living creatures and 24 elders who are singing new songs. Jesus is crowned with glory and honour, seated on the throne with the Father. We can only gaze in awe and wonder.

A series of songs praises the Lamb, first for rescuing his people so that they can be 'a kingdom and priests serving our God', and then for what he deserves, all the praise of which we are capable. The Lamb shares the praise that belongs to God. And now, set free through Jesus' sacrifice from the false idols that held us captive and prevented us from worshipping God, we are free to worship God and play our part in his purposes.

Spend some time meditating on this passage. Our true vocation is worshipping and serving God. How are you working out your vocation?

ROSIE WARD

What hath God wrought!

At the simplest level, technology (defined as 'techniques, skills, methods and processes used in the production of goods or services or in the accomplishment of objectives') may just be a tool. This doesn't have to be particularly new – the plough, sail and bridle all appear in the pages of scripture and have been used by humans for centuries. Increasingly, however, technologies are more complex and, with innovations in artificial intelligence and machines autonomous of human control, advancing technology presents society with new ethical dilemmas.

Each product of human ingenuity affects us and often the world around us. Sometimes this effect can be profound – changing the way we interact with each other and our environment or altering the way we view those with whom we come into contact, perhaps even the way that we think about God. We benefit greatly from technologies; where would many of us be without the medications that we take daily? Most of us would soon miss the technology that enables us to communicate effortlessly with friends and family over long distances.

As humans, we have the ability to use technology in ways that are constructive and helpful or that are destructive and harmful. The same technology brings us both nuclear power and the fearsome destructive power of nuclear weapons.

In 1970, the Church of Scotland recognised the profound effect technology often has on us, and so established the Society, Religion and Technology (SRT) Project, to help the church engage with ethical issues in science and technology. Since 2008, it has been my privilege to lead the SRT Project, and many of the reflections in this series are based on issues the project has considered.

Over the next few days, as we look at some of the ways in which technology impacts us as individuals, as people of faith and as communities, may we be filled again with a sense of thankfulness to God for the gifts that he gives and be spurred on afresh to be more effective servants of the one who calls us to be faithful. My hope is that you will be encouraged and blessed, and that God will be glorified, as we consider together some aspects of technology in the light of scripture.

MURDO MACDONALD

Called to redeem

Many peoples will come and say, 'Come, let us go up to the mountain of the Lord, to the temple of the God of Jacob. He will teach us his ways, so that we may walk in his paths.' The law will go out from Zion, the word of the Lord from Jerusalem. He will judge between the nations and will settle disputes for many peoples. They will beat their swords into ploughshares and their spears into pruning hooks. Nation will not take up sword against nation, nor will they train for war any more.

It is uncomfortable to reflect on how much technology has been driven by our human desire to dominate those around us or to achieve military superiority. Even some of the things we use every day – such as satellite navigation systems in our cars – have their origins in military technologies.

Fortunately, there are many examples of technology that was originally developed for war having been retooled for peaceful and humanitarian purposes. One such example is the drone or 'unmanned aerial vehicle' (UAV). Originally often mounted with weapons and designed to kill people, versions have now been developed for peaceful purposes, such as inspecting high buildings, searching for people lost during natural disasters or delivering medical supplies to remote health posts in Africa.

While it is a matter of shame and frustration that much human effort and resource continues to be expended in looking for new and 'more effective' ways of inflicting harm on others, this reflects our fallen human nature. As followers of Christ, we are called to a ministry of redemption. Jesus said, 'Blessed are the peacemakers' (Matthew 5:9).

Most of us won't be involved in 'training for war' in the military sense, but the words of today's passage remain relevant. We are called to beat metaphorical swords into ploughshares – to redeem the opportunities we are given, to bring about peace rather than conflict. We have opportunities not simply to disarm situations, but to use our efforts and ingenuity actively to retool things that can cause hurt (indeed, that may have been intentionally designed to do so), in order that peace, prosperity and flourishing may prevail instead.

Look for opportunities today to be faithful to our call to be peacemakers.

MURDO MACDONALD

Call to me

While Jeremiah was still confined in the courtyard of the guard, the word of the Lord came to him a second time: 'This is what the Lord says, he who made the earth, the Lord who formed it and established it – the Lord is his name: "Call to me and I will answer you and tell you great and unsearchable things you do not know."'

We live in a world where we seem to interact more and more with machines, whether through mobile phones, fitness trackers or increasingly automated cars. The ways in which we communicate with machines are not only increasing, but they are also evolving. Many of us are old enough to remember when we programmed computers using punch cards. I am typing this on a standard keyboard, but when I browse the internet I use a different form of interaction with a machine, pointing and clicking on links or icons, often using touch screens.

Even that is becoming outmoded – our house has at least half a dozen devices that connect to the internet by voice activation. Keyboards and touchscreens may soon become as obsolete as punch cards as we move towards other ways of interacting with machines – via gestures, emotions and perhaps, in the future, directly by thought.

Interacting with machines can often be used to augment and facilitate our communicating with other people; we have all experienced the benefits that this brings. Technology brings us many apps and opportunities to enrich our understanding of the Bible, to spur us on to more faithful and better-informed prayer and to broadcast the message of the gospel more widely, more efficiently and more cost-effectively.

However, as Jeremiah reminds us, at the heart of our faith is the need to commune with the living God. There are times when people and circumstances conspire to interrupt that communication. Our walk with God can be assisted and augmented using technology, but we need to take care that we don't allow the things of the world to interrupt our connection with our heavenly Father.

Lord, we are reassured that when we call to you, you will answer.

MURDO MACDONALD

Peace

Jesus replied, 'Anyone who loves me will obey my teaching. My Father will love them, and we will come to them and make our home with them... But the Advocate, the Holy Spirit, whom the Father will send in my name, will teach you all things and will remind you of everything I have said to you. Peace I leave with you; my peace I give you. I do not give to you as the world gives. Do not let your hearts be troubled and do not be afraid.'

Many of us will recognise the scene: a family sitting together, each interacting not with those around them but with their own tablet, phone or laptop. On the bus or train, commuters are in their own worlds, headphones cutting them off from the sounds around them.

It is ironic that in a society where, equipped with electronic devices, we are more connected than ever, many of us are marooned from those closest to us. Wi-Fi and social media bring benefits, allowing communities that would otherwise not have existed to flourish, but there is a downside to being always connected. This is perhaps especially evident with younger people, where FOMO (fear of missing out) keeps many wedded to their phones in ways widely acknowledged to be detrimental to mental health.

Where among all that clamours for our attention – email, text messages, Facebook posts – do we find this peace Jesus talks of? Just as Jesus sought time alone with God, we need to seek the peace that he talks about. Perhaps we should consider a 'digital detox', taking a sabbath rest from electronic communications, or consciously decide to pick up our Bibles before we pick up our mobile phones in the morning?

Jesus' words here are bracketed by assurances in relation to all three persons of the Trinity: we can be at peace because God's people are promised that the Spirit, the Comforter, will be with us; though Jesus is currently absent from us in the body, he is coming back; and when he returns, he will take us to be with his Father.

Technology and the 'always connected' culture may militate against it, but we are called to seek Christ's peace – a transcending peace, which we must share with the world.

MURDO MACDONALD

Food is a gift from God

The Lord your God is bringing you into a good land – a land with brooks, streams, and deep springs gushing out into the valleys and hills; a land with wheat and barley, vines and fig-trees, pomegranates, olive oil and honey... When you have eaten and are satisfied, praise the Lord your God for the good land he has given you. Be careful that you do not forget the Lord your God, failing to observe his commands, his laws and his decrees... But remember the Lord your God, for it is he who gives you the ability to produce wealth, and so confirms his covenant, which he swore to your ancestors, as it is today.

To a large extent, augmented by technology, farming in developed countries has been transformed into an industry. This has brought great benefits – through the use of fertilisers, we can now grow much more per hectare; selective breeding means that each animal is more productive; robots are able to remove weeds more effectively; food can be preserved and safely transported from all corners of the globe.

As a consequence, many people have access to more than enough food. However, it is to our shame that while there is enough food to provide for all humanity, the unequal sharing of this bounty means that more than 800 million people (one person in every nine) will go to bed hungry tonight and that one in three people are malnourished.

The agrarian society of Bible times meant that most people retained an intimate connection with food production. Many of us in modern western society, far removed from the production of what we eat, have largely lost a connection that previous generations had. We no longer live in fear that a bad harvest or a lack of rainfall may mean we will struggle to provide for our families through the lean winter months.

As we mark the beginning of Lent, could we see this as an opportunity to moderate or change our consumption of food so that others can benefit?

Heavenly Father, we are reminded that we are ultimately dependent on your gracious hand to sustain us. Help us never to forget that you supply all our needs and to remember those for whom every day is a struggle to survive.

MURDO MACDONALD

Striving together: celebrating competitiveness in sport

Do you not know that in a race all the runners run, but only one gets the prize? Run in such a way as to get the prize. Everyone who competes in the games goes into strict training. They do it to get a crown that will not last; but we do it to get a crown that will last for ever. Therefore I do not run like someone running aimlessly.

Whether it's a carbon-fibre tennis racket, the aerofoil on a Formula 1 racing car or the carefully controlled dietary regime of the elite athlete, technology has a huge influence on sport. Many sports use technologies to check whether a score has been made or a batsman is out.

Most of us will never aspire to compete in sport at the elite level, yet, as Paul reminds us, competition is a natural and healthy part of human life. We compete for jobs or resources, and we vie to get attention for our endeavours through our church websites or ads in the local paper. There may even be times when our churches are in competition with each other!

Competition can – perhaps should – be healthy. As the writer of Proverbs reminds us, 'As iron sharpens iron, so one person sharpens another' (Proverbs 27:17). We can gain much from competing, which in turn makes us better prepared for the next challenge.

However, we may sometimes feel that competitiveness is wrong, and there are certainly times when cooperation is the better approach. When we compete, as followers of Christ we should ensure that we respect those with whom we are competing. How often, in describing those who follow another team (or belong to another church), do we denigrate or seek to humiliate them or show them in a less flattering light? We need to stay within the rules – 'gamesmanship' or manipulation of the rules are not glorifying to God – and, in every sphere of life, the glory of God should be our ultimate focus.

Christ's divinity and humanity were in competition in the garden of Gethsemane – 'Yet not as I will, but as you will' (Matthew 26:39). How does this daily struggle play out in our lives?

MURDO MACDONALD

Energy issues and fuel poverty

What good is it, my brothers and sisters, if someone claims to have faith but has no deeds? Can such faith save them? Suppose a brother or a sister is without clothes and daily food. If one of you says to them, 'Go in peace; keep warm and well fed,' but does nothing about their physical needs, what good is it? In the same way, faith by itself, if it is not accompanied by action, is dead.

For many of us, central heating and constant access to hot water are part of normal life. However, it is to our shame that, even in our affluent societies, there are families who face the daily choice of whether to 'heat or eat'– they simply cannot afford the luxury of being both warm and well fed. Fuel poverty in the UK is defined as having to spend more than 10% of your income in order to keep warm; it is estimated that over four million households in the UK – that's one household in every six – fall into this category. This can have devastating consequences for the health and well-being of those affected, especially the young and the old. When we encounter people in this position, is our response to say in effect, 'Go in peace'?

In today's reading, James reminds us that this dilemma is nothing new – at the time that the New Testament was being written, many were destitute and, without the social-security safety net we have become accustomed to, were in need of practical help. James urges the followers of Christ to demonstrate their faith by responding to this need with more than just kind words and comforting thoughts – or even with their prayers or spiritual support. While all of these are of vital importance, we are called to take practical steps – to do something about the physical needs of those we encounter.

Many churches respond by providing help in practical ways. The physical needs of our brothers and sisters are important; James reminds us that it's not unspiritual to be concerned about these.

If one in every six homes in your parish or community lives in fuel poverty, how many people would that affect? What action could you take, either as an individual or a church?

MURDO MACDONALD

Asteroseismology

The heavens declare the glory of God; the skies proclaim the work of his hands. Day after day they pour forth speech; night after night they reveal knowledge. They have no speech, they use no words; no sound is heard from them. Yet their voice goes out into all the earth, their words to the ends of the world.

It's safe to say that the academic discipline of asteroseismology is one that most of us (including me!) are largely unfamiliar with. However, the realisation that we can study the sounds that stars make, and that outer space isn't as silent as we had previously thought, is one of the unexpected outcomes of human space exploration.

I have to confess that, reading today's familiar passage from the Psalms, I had often presumed that the writer was using allegorical language or poetic licence. However, as the technology of our spacecraft has developed, we have recently been privileged to listen in to what is happening as comets hurtle through space and as moons orbit planets such as Saturn.

Through our exploration of space, we as mortal humans have come to understand more fully our place in the universe. An unexpected side-effect of this is the discovery that there is a real sense in which the heavenly bodies 'pour forth speech' in praise of God. No words (in the conventional understanding) are used, of course. As Paul reminds us, sometimes we too find ourselves praying without words: 'the Spirit himself intercedes for us through wordless groans' (Romans 8:26).

Scientific discoveries such as these astound us. While we are undoubtedly in the early stages of exploring the universe around us, the ability to appreciate the 'songs of the stars' (as some of the scientists studying these phenomena have described what they hear) serves as a reminder of the fact that the glory of God is sometimes hidden in plain sight.

Technology can draw us closer to God in unexpected ways; science sometimes gives us a profound insight into what God is saying to us through the Bible and through the glories of his creation.

As we observe the majesty of your creation, help us, O Lord, to glorify you.

MURDO MACDONALD

You are being watched!

The angel of the Lord also said to [Hagar]: 'You are now pregnant and you will give birth to a son. You shall name him Ishmael, for the Lord has heard of your misery...' She gave this name to the Lord who spoke to her: 'You are the God who sees me,' for she said, 'I have now seen the One who sees me.'

We live in a world where we are frequently under observation. Sometimes we are aware of this – speed cameras on roads or security cameras in shops, for example. At other times, we don't fully appreciate the extent to which our movements and actions are tracked. If we have a mobile phone in our pocket or wear a fitness tracker, our position can be determined, often to within a few feet.

Much of the data collected on us is in digital format. This means that information from multiple sources – electronic transactions, internet searches or medical records – can easily be amalgamated and analysed. For some, this raises concerns that this information may be misused or misinterpreted, perhaps to exclude or marginalise.

While digital surveillance may be a modern phenomenon, observation is not new. It can be carried out for protective or benevolent purposes, for example, in order to protect people or property. There are many instances in scripture where God is talked of as watching over his people in order to protect, such as in Psalm 23, where the image is of a shepherd watching over his flock. At other times, such as in Psalm 139, God's gaze is altogether more penetrating: 'Search me, God... See if there is any offensive way in me' (vv. 23–24). However, as our God is one who cares for and loves us, we can be comforted by his all-knowing gaze.

Although marginalised by society for multiple reasons (as a foreigner, a slave and a woman), Hagar, the only woman in the Old Testament who gives a name to God ('the One who sees me'), was comforted by his caring gaze. We too can be reassured that God sees, God hears and God cares – even for those on the margins or who are excluded from our society.

Loving Father, thank you that we can know that you see us and care for us.

MURDO MACDONALD

Who should be able to see my thoughts?

For the word of God is alive and active. Sharper than any double-edged sword, it penetrates even to dividing soul and spirit, joints and marrow; it judges the thoughts and attitudes of the heart. Nothing in all creation is hidden from God's sight. Everything is uncovered and laid bare before the eyes of him to whom we must give account.

Neuroscience now allows access to that most complex of organs, the human brain. Through technologies such as magnetic resonance imaging (MRI) we can observe what is going on inside people's heads as it happens. However, impressive and enlightening as this is, what brain scans show us are not the thoughts themselves but the increased blood flow that indicates brain activity associated with these thoughts.

Nor are we limited to simply observing what is going on inside our brains – we can manipulate the brain as well. We have long used chemical or surgical interventions; more recently we have been applying other approaches, even succeeding in experimentally implanting false memories in lab animals such as mice and rats.

However, although there is much that this can teach us about the physical aspects of ourselves, we are more than simply the sum of our physical parts. Theology and philosophy are also essential to understanding what humans really are; what we are is in relation to the creator God.

A Christian understanding of who we are can be informed by advances in neurobiology. These discoveries may also be helpful in clarifying the philosophical and ethical debates regarding freedom, autonomy, sin and moral responsibility. But the Christian characterisation of human persons and their responsibility confers on them a value and dignity that cannot be reduced merely to the material – to what we can observe or measure.

As humans, we transcend the created universe and are able to communicate with the uncreated God, the source of all love and free will. This is a mystery beyond all measure – one for which we can all be truly thankful.

'What a person is on their knees before God, that he is – and nothing more'
(Robert Murray McCheyene, 1813–43).

MURDO MACDONALD

Caring comes first

Jesus said: 'A man was going down from Jerusalem to Jericho, when he was attacked by robbers. They stripped him of his clothes, beat him and went away, leaving him half-dead... A Samaritan... came where the man was; and when he saw him, he took pity on him. He went to him and bandaged his wounds, pouring on oil and wine. Then he put the man on his own donkey, brought him to an inn and took care of him.

The use of technology in healthcare, as in other areas of life, is increasing exponentially, bringing great benefit to many. Where would we be without X-rays and other imaging technologies? And many of us walk around with replacement parts in our bodies, whether hip joints or heart valves.

However, we mustn't lose sight of how important 'care' is in 'healthcare'. As we deploy more and better technology in the context of healthcare, there is a concern that this can distance us from each other, and thus cause us to potentially lose sight of the need to show care and compassion.

While it brings great benefits, there is a danger that technology comes between us as people, meaning that society and community become more fragmented. We need to ensure that everyone in our society is cared for and that technologies are deployed not in ways that disadvantage or exclude, but rather to help us all connect more effectively and understand our humanity more deeply.

As people of faith, Christians affirm the importance of being part of community and society. A pivotal aspect of community involves caring for each other. When Jesus told the story in today's passage, he described how the despised Samaritan not only made use of the available medical and transport technology of the day (bandages, oil and wine for the assaulted man's wounds; a donkey to carry him to the inn), but he also 'took care of him' (v. 34). We, too, are called to use the means at our disposal to ensure that caring comes first.

Give thanks for those who use their skills to care for others, and pray that we too may care for all with whom we come in contact today.

MURDO MACDONALD

Healing and wholeness

Now Abraham moved on from there into the region of the Negev...
There Abraham said of his wife Sarah, 'She is my sister.' Then Abimelek
king of Gerar sent for Sarah and took her... Then Abraham prayed to
God, and God healed Abimelek, his wife and his female slaves so they
could have children again, for the Lord had kept all the women in
Abimelek's household from conceiving because of Abraham's wife
Sarah.

The role of an editor involves making changes – to alter the words of a
newspaper article or book chapter to make it easier to understand and
free from mistakes. Remarkably, humans now have the ability to do
something similar with living organisms. Genome-editing technology
gives us the opportunity to change the genetic code that determines
many aspects of how an organism functions. Scientists have been able to
do this in plants and various simple animals for some time; the same
technology is now being applied to humans.

A recent meeting that I attended brought together scientists, theologi-
ans, ethicists and lawyers to discuss the ethical implications of this technology. One of the questions that arose was 'What does it mean to be
human?' If we can alter the DNA of another individual, does that put us in
a godlike role of being able to fundamentally change another person, one
who is made in the image of God?

These discussions lead to questions around healing and wholeness.
Healing was a large part of Jesus' earthly ministry, and there is a sense in
which salvation restores the broken image of God in us to wholeness.

The story in Genesis 20 is one that makes us uncomfortable, as people
interact in ways we find distressing. However, it is remarkable for a number
of reasons, including the fact that this is the first recorded example in scripture of healing. And what an example! The extent of God's grace is shown:
the recipients of the healing – necessary because Abraham, the friend of
God (James 2:23), failed to trust God – encompasses the slaves of a
Philistine king. God's grace is so much wider than we can ever imagine.

Loving Lord, we thank you that you are the ever-gracious healer.

MURDO MACDONALD

Transplantation

'Then the righteous will answer him, "Lord, when did we see you hungry and feed you, or thirsty and give you something to drink? When did we see you a stranger and invite you in, or needing clothes and clothe you? When did we see you ill or in prison and go to visit you?" The King will reply, "Truly I tell you, whatever you did for one of the least of these brothers and sisters of mine, you did for me."'

The ability to transplant organs and tissues from one person to another has meant that the lives of many people have been improved immeasurably, and in many cases significantly extended. Many families are thankful to others who, often at a time of great tragedy, have been willing to allow a variety of tissues and organs to be removed from a loved one, in order that these can give life and hope to an unrelated person in need.

In the UK, as in many western countries, the supply of organs for transplantation is dependent on a system of voluntary donation. This is not without its problems; some, perhaps for religious reasons, are uncomfortable with the concept of organ donation. In addition, as I write, there is debate as to whether to move to a system where, in the absence of any other objection, organs are assumed to be available for transplantation.

Clearly, at the time when Jesus spoke the words in today's reading, the technology to allow such life-saving operations to take place did not exist. However, many have seen a parallel between the sacrificial giving to which Christ's followers are called and our using the resources at our disposal to help others. In the words of the great Methodist preacher John Wesley, we are called to 'do all the good you can, by all the means you can, in all the ways you can, in all the places you can, at all the times you can, to all the people you can, as long as ever you can' – perhaps even after we have died.

The fleshandblood campaign is an interdenominational effort 'to mobilise the people and resources of the church to help increase the number of blood and organ donors'. Do you feel this resonates with Jesus' call to his followers to remember 'the least of these'?

MURDO MACDONALD

Family ties

Ram was the father of Amminadab, and Amminadab the father of Nahshon, the leader of the people of Judah. Nahshon was the father of Salmon, Salmon the father of Boaz, Boaz the father of Obed and Obed the father of Jesse. Jesse was the father of Eliab… Abinadab… Shimea… Nethanel… Raddai… Ozem and… David. Their sisters were Zeruiah and Abigail. Zeruiah's three sons were Abishai, Joab and Asahel. Abigail was the mother of Amasa, whose father was Jether the Ishmaelite.

However enthusiastic we may be about the Bible, for most of us, if we're honest, our hearts sink when we come across some parts of scripture. This may be because we find them uncomfortable (such as psalms that invoke judgement or curses on enemies), irrelevant (all those details of how the tabernacle was constructed) or just plain boring.

Genealogies are bits of the Bible we're often tempted to skip over – how does this impact our lives in the 21st century? There are about two dozen of these lists of names, most in the Old Testament but also some in the gospels of Matthew and Luke. The one in today's passage is unusual in that it records the names of not just sons but also some daughters.

As I write, the 40th anniversary of the birth of the first 'test tube baby' has recently been marked. It is estimated that over six million children have now been born as a result of similar medical interventions and that assisted-reproductive technologies are thought to play a part in 2% of all live births in the UK. This has profound implications for society and for the church, not least in terms of pastoral care.

This ability to intervene at the earliest stage of human development has changed the way that society thinks about relatedness and about how we build families. However, our interrelatedness remains important. While the context was very different in biblical times, in the pages of scripture we see illustrated various family structures – some of which are reflected in the genealogies.

For many, family life may not be as we would wish. Remember those known to you who may struggle; pray also for those whose struggle may be known only to God.

MURDO MACDONALD

End of life

Abraham lived a hundred and seventy-five years. Then Abraham breathed his last and died at a good old age, an old man and full of years; and he was gathered to his people. His sons Isaac and Ishmael buried him in the cave of Machpelah near Mamre, in the field of Ephron son of Zohar the Hittite, the field Abraham had bought from the Hittites. There Abraham was buried with his wife Sarah.

Old age is a gift, but even with the best of modern medical care, few of us can expect to come close to the great age Abraham achieved. (I can't help a wry smile when, in Genesis 47:9, Abraham's grandson Jacob describes his own 130 years as being 'few and difficult'.) Life expectancy in many societies continues to rise: experts predict that the average child born in a developed country today can expect to live to be 100.

Humans have long dreamed of cheating death, of achieving physical immortality – serious scientific experiments have attempted this. However, although technological intervention can postpone the inevitable, as Benjamin Franklin quipped, death and taxes remain life's only certainties.

In western culture, many are uncomfortable with death, and it can be difficult to encourage people to face up to its inevitability. This discomfort can sometimes be reinforced by modern medicine – there can be a sense that every death represents a medical failure, rather than accepting that death is a normal part of life. It is necessary to recognise that there are times when ensuring comfort during a final illness is more appropriate than repeated life-prolonging interventions.

This passage is a beautiful example of a life well lived and a death well died. Scripture makes it clear that Abraham was far from perfect, and the story of the fractured relationship between his two sons makes painful reading. Yet, as we read here, at the end Isaac and Ishmael, bitter rivals for the promises of the covenant, came together to honour and mourn for their father and to bury him with the wife he loved.

We can all learn lessons from a good death, while affirming and celebrating the benefits medical technologies bring. Pray for those who mourn.

MURDO MACDONALD

Gardens in the Bible

When I first started to think about what passages might be included under the heading 'Gardens in the Bible', it seemed that the list might be embarrassingly short. Yes, we have the garden of Eden and the garden of Gethsemane – but then what? I was struggling.

I needn't have worried. A quick glance at my concordance revealed a wealth of material of great variety and nuance; indeed, there are many more examples than can be encompassed within a fortnight of reflections. We will begin with Eden in Genesis, move through the Bible in roughly book order and conclude with the tree of life in the New Jerusalem in Revelation. With a couple of references I have stretched the definition slightly, in that while the term 'garden' is not explicitly used, the passage nevertheless involves landscape and growth in some form.

The garden forms the backdrop to a great variety of themes and ideas. A garden is the setting of humanity's first disobedience and loss (Genesis 3:1–7). A healthy garden is presented as a symbol of good and wise stewardship (Proverbs 27:23–27; 28:19). Possession of a garden is flaunted to conspicuously display wealth (Ecclesiastes 2:5–6). A garden is used as a metaphor for a place of consolation after a time of trial and testing (Isaiah 51:1–3) or as a place where one can put down deep roots and grow in stability (Jeremiah 29:4–7). Negatively, a garden is a place of acute personal challenge and betrayed friendship (Matthew 26:36–41, 47–56), but ultimately, the garden is a symbol of hope and promise for the future (Revelation 2:7; 22:1–2).

As we reflect on these passages over the next two weeks, it may be helpful to consider the role of the various 'garden' experiences in our own lives. In John 15:1–11, Jesus refers to his Father as the gardener, or vinegrower; are we willing to submit to his pruning and redirection, rather than stubbornly persist down our own chosen path? If we can, we will be able to embrace with confidence the promise that we shall be 'like a watered garden... whose waters never fail' (Isaiah 58:11, NRSV).

BARBARA MOSSE

79

Paradise lost

Now the serpent was more crafty than any other wild animal that the Lord God had made. He said to the woman, 'Did God say, "You shall not eat from any tree in the garden"?' The woman said… 'We may eat of the fruit of the trees in the garden; but God said, "You shall not eat of the fruit of the tree that is in the middle of the garden, nor shall you touch it, or you shall die."' But the serpent said… 'You will not die; for God knows that when you eat of it your eyes will be opened, and you will be like God, knowing good and evil.' So… she took of its fruit and ate; and… gave some to her husband… and he ate. Then the eyes of both were opened, and they knew that they were naked.

The whole drama of the creation and its evolving relationship with God is pictured as beginning in perhaps the most famous of all biblical gardens – Eden. Today's passage comes roughly halfway through the second creation account (Genesis 2—3) and immediately after the reference to humanity's original innocence (2:25). Into this state of paradisal bliss, the arrival of the 'crafty serpent', also created by God (3:1), comes as a rude intrusion. For the woman an element of doubt is planted ('Did God *really* say…?'), and disturbing, enticing new possibilities are introduced. The temptation proves irresistible; the fruit is eaten and the rest, so the saying goes, is history.

The temptation to eat the fruit remains. Recently, a number of articles have appeared concerning the growth of artificial intelligence and its increasing impact on our lives. Obviously much of this is good, but some people are warning that we aren't sufficiently aware of the possible consequences for humankind with the technology we are developing. Machines with the capacity to think for themselves – ultimately – may not 'need' human beings at all. Those looking ahead to possible consequences warn that our spiritual, emotional and moral capacity lags far behind our intellectual ability.

Can the events in the garden of Eden help us with today's temptations? Should there be limits to our intellectual striving? If so, are we able to discern where those limits should be?

BARBARA MOSSE

Echoes of Eden

You shall love the Lord your God, therefore, and keep his charge, his decrees, his ordinances, and his commandments always... Keep, then, this entire commandment that I am commanding you today... so that you may live long in the land that the Lord swore to your ancestors to give to them and their descendants, a land flowing with milk and honey. For the land that you are about to enter to occupy is not like the land of Egypt, from which you have come, where you sow your seed and irrigate by foot like a vegetable garden. But the land you are crossing over to occupy is a land of hills and valleys, watered by rain from the sky, a land that the Lord your God looks after.

We have come a long way from the garden of Eden. Adam and Eve's disobedience led to their expulsion from the garden, and their subsequent experience was toil and hardship (Genesis 3:14–24). But their descendants now stand on the threshold of the promised land. The picture painted by Moses as he describes the land the people are about to enter suggests a return to a pre-fall Eden. It is 'a land flowing with milk and honey' (v. 9) and 'a land of hills and valleys, watered by rain from the sky' (v. 11). His words also imply that the people won't have to struggle to survive, because it is 'a land that the Lord your God looks after' (v. 12).

But there is a condition. At the beginning of the passage and throughout the wider narrative, there is a repeated command to love God and keep his commandments, so that the people may prosper in their new home. The writers of these stories knew the reality of sin. They knew through long and bitter experience how human nature tends to lean away from what is in its best interests, towards weakness, failure and betrayal. The spiritual imperative to put God first never slips, and it continues throughout the Hebrew scriptures and on into the New Testament (Matthew 6:33).

How do you seek to live out this command to love and obey God first in your own life? And how do you see it being fulfilled – or not – in your experience of local and national church life?

BARBARA MOSSE

Nurture with care

Know well the condition of your flocks, and give attention to your herds; for riches do not last for ever, nor a crown for all generations. When the grass is gone, and new growth appears… the lambs will provide your clothing, and the goats the price of a field; there will be enough goats' milk for your food, for the food of your household… Anyone who tills the land will have plenty of bread, but one who follows worthless pursuits will have plenty of poverty.

The advice in this passage works well on various levels. It works locally, exhorting the farmer to care for his flocks and work hard in the fields, resulting in good provision for his family and household. It also works on a national level (see the reference to a crown in 27:24), with a king caring for his land and people. Either way, the speaker urges wise stewardship and thought for the future. We may wonder how this teaching from the Hebrew Bible sits alongside Jesus' later teaching to have no thought for tomorrow (Matthew 6:25–34), but the texts are dealing with completely different situations. Jesus is warning against a neurotic, fretful anxiety that fails to trust in God's care and provision; he is *not* discouraging an attitude of sensible, responsible stewardship.

Applying this teaching in our own circumstances shouldn't be too difficult. Whatever our situation, there will be something for which or somebody for whom we have a duty of love and care. We may have home and family responsibilities, and relationships with friends and colleagues need nurturing. Our God-given gifts and talents also need to be nurtured, not buried in the ground as the 'wicked and lazy' slave did with his talent in the parable (Matthew 25:14–30). We may find ways in which this teaching applies to our own lifestyle. Are we perhaps living 'on the hoof', with a need to slow down, take stock and make some provision for the future? Or perhaps the challenge is on a more personal level: are we able to acknowledge that God has gifted each of us in wonderful ways – and allow those gifts to be nurtured?

'I praise you, for I am fearfully and wonderfully made' (Psalm 139:14).

BARBARA MOSSE

More than enough

I said to myself, 'Come now, I will make a test of pleasure; enjoy yourself'… I made great works; I built houses and planted vineyards for myself; I made myself gardens and parks, and planted in them all kinds of fruit trees. I made myself pools from which to water the forest of growing trees. I bought male and female slaves, and had slaves who were born in my house; I also had great possessions of herds and flocks, more than any who had been before me in Jerusalem.

Here we have a shift in emphasis, and this cautionary tale from Ecclesiastes begins with a grand vision. Hard work is involved, certainly, in the building of houses, the planting of vineyards and the creation of parks and gardens – although it will almost certainly not be the speaker who is doing all the hard graft! Unlike yesterday's text, this work is not for the purpose of survival. This passage resonates with greed and with excess for the sake of excess, rather than conveying any sense of scraping a living or a hand-to-mouth existence. The speaker glories in his wealth, parading it gloatingly before his neighbours. It is 'a test of pleasure' (v. 1), a deliberate exercise in competitive consumption.

Does this sound familiar? We may, perhaps, find ourselves comparing the outlook of the speaker in this passage with the antics of some of the super-rich in our society, vying among themselves to be the owner of the latest – and largest – super yacht. We may think of certain bankers who take huge bonuses for themselves even as their institutions fail and many thousands of ordinary savers suffer badly in consequence. When we think of such examples, we may be tempted to pat ourselves on the back, like the Pharisee in Jesus' parable – 'God, I thank you that I am not like other people: thieves, rogues, adulterers, or even like this tax-collector' (Luke 18:11). We may congratulate ourselves with the belief that we would never behave like that. But is this true? What about our attitude to our own possessions, however plentiful or few?

'Create in me a clean heart, O God, and put a new and right spirit within me' (Psalm 51:10).

BARBARA MOSSE

Return to the source

Listen to me, you that pursue righteousness, you that seek the Lord. Look to the rock from which you were hewn, and to the quarry from which you were dug. Look to Abraham your father and to Sarah who bore you; for he was but one when I called him, but I blessed him and made him many. For the Lord will comfort Zion; he will comfort all her waste places, and will make her wilderness like Eden, her desert like the garden of the Lord; joy and gladness will be found in her, thanksgiving and the voice of song.

Here are words of enormous comfort for the people of Israel, who are in exile far from their homeland. In their discouragement, the words of the prophet urge them to 'look to the rock from which [they] were hewn, and to the quarry from which [they] were dug'. These are hard, graphic images, and the process of birth is never easy or pain-free. But the Israelites are the descendants of Abraham and Sarah, the prophet reminds them, and are therefore the children of God's promise.

And that promise will continue to be fulfilled, despite the Israelites' present hardships. The Lord will bring 'comfort' and 'will make her wilderness like Eden, her desert like the garden of the Lord' (v. 3). Again, the promise is for a restoration of the lost paradise of Eden. In some of our earlier passages the garden has been a place of hard and bitter toil; here, God is the gardener, creating a place of beauty, refreshment and joy for his people.

When we are in a dark place, it's not always easy to see the light at the end of the tunnel. At such times this prophecy of Isaiah is as much for us as for the ancient Israelites; we, too, are urged – encouraged – to look to the source of our calling. Because the God who calls us is faithful, and although our outward circumstances may not seem to change much, our trust in God's presence with us in those circumstances makes all the difference.

'Even though I walk through the darkest valley, I fear no evil; for you are with me; your rod and your staff – they comfort me' (Psalm 23:4).

BARBARA MOSSE

Like a watered garden

If you remove the yoke from among you, the pointing of the finger, the speaking of evil, if you offer your food to the hungry and satisfy the needs of the afflicted, then your light shall rise in the darkness and your gloom be like the noonday. The Lord will guide you continually, and satisfy your needs in parched places, and make your bones strong; and you shall be like a watered garden, like a spring of water, whose waters never fail.

Isaiah's prophecy moves on from the realm of general principles to the more specific concerns of everyday life. The prophet's words again are full of hope and promise, but they also reveal a keen insight into human nature: 'If you remove the yoke from among you, the pointing of the finger, the speaking of evil, if you offer your food to the hungry and satisfy the needs of the afflicted…' (vv. 9–10). The writer unerringly pinpoints two troubling human weaknesses: the temptation to indulge in spiteful gossip and criticism; and the selfish desire to hoard the good things we have and resist sharing them with others. And with these words of Isaiah the centuries are rolled back, because the weaknesses he identifies are with us still.

Despite the passage of the centuries and the huge changes in life experience, human nature itself does not change. The problems identified by Isaiah will be recognisable within any gathering of people today, and probably, if we are honest, within ourselves. God doesn't offer us a magic-wand solution to human problems. The darkness and the gloom will not instantly be removed, but the reassurance offered is that God will continually be present in the darkness, transforming it with mysterious light. And that presence is nurturing, quenching the soul's thirst so that it will become like a watered garden, 'like a spring of water, whose waters never fail' (v. 11). The anticipation here of Jesus' 'spring of water gushing up to eternal life' (John 4:14) is unmistakeable.

Find some time to sit quietly with God today. Trust in his continual presence, ask and receive his forgiveness and allow him to 'satisfy your needs in parched places'.

BARBARA MOSSE

Blossoming into wholeness

I will greatly rejoice in the Lord, my whole being shall exult in my God; for he has clothed me with the garments of salvation, he has covered me with the robe of righteousness, as a bridegroom decks himself with a garland, and as a bride adorns herself with her jewels. For as the earth brings forth its shoots, and as a garden causes what is sown in it to spring up, so the Lord God will cause righteousness and praise to spring up before all the nations. For Zion's sake I will not keep silent, and for Jerusalem's sake I will not rest, until her vindication shines out like the dawn, and her salvation like a burning torch.

In our reflections so far, we have seen that the image of a garden is used in scripture with a kaleidoscope of meanings, and today's passage offers yet another perspective. Here the teaching seems to be aimed at the nation of Israel as a whole. The prophet uses a well-tended garden as a metaphor for a well-ordered society – one that has the praise and worship of God at its heart; one that functions with God's righteousness and justice; one that truly is 'a light for revelation to the Gentiles' (Luke 2:32).

The image of a garden is a symbol of faith, hope and trust. The gardener plants the seed, trusting that the mysterious processes that go on invisibly within the darkness of the soil will, in time, bring the plant to glorious fruition. He can't witness the transformation occurring, and any attempt to do so would probably kill it.

Jesus himself referred to this mysterious process in his own teaching (Mark 4:26–29). If Israel would only tend to its life and relationship with God with the same care and attention that a conscientious gardener brings to his work, then that life of justice and righteousness would indeed blossom 'before all the nations'.

Reflect for a few moments today on how helpful – or not – you find this particular use of the garden image in your own context. Does it have anything to say in relation to your experience of church fellowship? To what you see in the life of the national church?

BARBARA MOSSE

In for the long haul

Thus says the Lord of hosts, the God of Israel, to all the exiles whom I have sent into exile from Jerusalem to Babylon: Build houses and live in them; plant gardens and eat what they produce. Take wives and have sons and daughters; take wives for your sons, and give your daughters in marriage, that they may bear sons and daughters; multiply there, and do not decrease. But seek the welfare of the city where I have sent you into exile, and pray to the Lord on its behalf, for in its welfare you will find your welfare.

The exile of almost the entire Israelite nation to Babylon was experienced as an unmitigated disaster by the people. They had lost the land that God had given them and with it the holy city of Jerusalem and its temple, the dwelling place of God on earth. The opening words of Psalm 137 capture their despair perfectly: 'By the rivers of Babylon – there we sat down and there we wept when we remembered Zion.' Jeremiah the prophet was one of the few who had remained behind in Jerusalem, and today's passage contains an extract from his letter to the exiles. It contains some rather surprising advice.

First, the people are to stop looking back to the past and grieving for what cannot be undone. God is still in charge, and God is actively and positively working through what has happened. Then, trusting in God, they are to put down roots in Babylon; they are to build houses, plant gardens, have children and see those children raise children of their own.

All these activities involve time and patience. The growth of a mature garden can't be rushed, despite the proliferation of quick-fix gardening programmes on television!

Patience in adversity is not something that comes easily to us, and when things go wrong I'm sure we can all identify with the desire to turn back the clock. When in a crisis, are we able to consider Jeremiah's approach? His message suggests that our present trouble is being used by God to fulfil a much deeper, long-term purpose for our good.

'Then Job answered the Lord: "I know that you can do all things, and that no purpose of yours can be thwarted"' (Job 42:1–2).

BARBARA MOSSE

A new creation

For I am about to create new heavens and a new earth; the former things shall not be remembered or come to mind. But be glad and rejoice for ever in what I am creating; for I am about to create Jerusalem as a joy, and its people as a delight. I will rejoice in Jerusalem, and delight in my people; no more shall the sound of weeping be heard in it, or the cry of distress. No more shall there be in it an infant that lives but a few days, or an old person who does not live out a lifetime... They shall build houses and inhabit them; they shall plant vineyards and eat their fruit. They shall not build and another inhabit; they shall not plant and another eat; for like the days of a tree shall the days of my people be, and my chosen shall long enjoy the work of their hands.

Another prophet – this time Isaiah – speaks words of prophetic hope into the despair of the exiles in Babylon. This passage has a lot in common with the words of Jeremiah we were considering yesterday: houses will be built and their builders will continue to live in them; vineyards will be planted and the gardeners will eat the fruits of their own labours.

But where Jeremiah addressed the plight of the newly arrived exiles in Babylon directly, Isaiah looks further ahead to a future they can scarcely imagine. This prophecy relates to the end times and the fulfilment of God's ultimate purposes. Isaiah's vision speaks of 'new heavens and a new earth' (v. 17) and the new Jerusalem as 'a joy' (v. 18). There will be peace and prosperity and no untimely death.

How seriously are we able to take these prophecies in relation to our own lives? The constant bombardment of bad news that comes at us 24 hours a day is often overwhelming, and it may be hard to imagine any phoenix being able to rise out of the ashes. How deep is our trust in God? Are we able to believe that God can work in all our life experience, even in the darkest areas?

'Even the darkness is not dark to you; the night is as bright as the day, for darkness is as light to you' (Psalm 139:12).

BARBARA MOSSE

Garden of agony

Then Jesus went with them to a place called Gethsemane; and he said to his disciples, 'Sit here while I go over there and pray.' He took with him Peter and the two sons of Zebedee, and began to be grieved and agitated. Then he said to them, 'I am deeply grieved, even to death; remain here, and stay awake with me.' And going a little farther, he threw himself on the ground and prayed, 'My Father, if it is possible, let this cup pass from me; yet not what I want but what you want.' Then he came to the disciples and found them sleeping; and he said to Peter, 'So, could you not stay awake with me one hour? Stay awake and pray that you may not come into the time of trial; the spirit indeed is willing, but the flesh is weak.'

After Eden, the garden of Gethsemane is perhaps the most famous garden in scripture, and we come to it now at the ultimate moment of crisis for Jesus. It is the night before his crucifixion, and Jesus wrestles with the supreme horror of what he knows lies ahead of him. Seeking some support, he takes Peter, James and John with him into the garden, telling them to pray while he communes privately with his Father. If we continue reading for a few verses on from today's passage, we see that Jesus has to make this request three times, and each time the disciples fall asleep.

What was Jesus expecting – hoping for – when he invited Peter, James and John into the garden with him? Clearly, he was looking for support and encouragement in his time of extreme testing, and it is in the garden of Gethsemane that we find Jesus at his most vulnerable. 'My Father,' he prayed, 'if it is possible, let this cup pass from me.' Three times Jesus looked for support – and three times he was disappointed. Yet Jesus understood human frailty: 'the spirit indeed is willing, but the flesh is weak' (v. 41). He knew, ultimately, where his true support was to come from.

Human support can only go so far. When we are in difficulty, do we sometimes expect too much of others? Are we looking for help in the right place?

BARBARA MOSSE

Judgement and mercy

Then [Jesus] told this parable: 'A man had a fig tree planted in his vine-yard; and he came looking for fruit on it and found none. So he said to the gardener, "See here! For three years I have come looking for fruit on this fig tree, and still I find none. Cut it down! Why should it be wasting the soil?" He replied, "Sir, let it alone for one more year, until I dig it round and put manure on it. If it bears fruit next year, well and good; but if not, you can cut it down."'

This parable of Jesus forms part of a slightly longer piece (Luke 13:1–9) that is concerned with the question of repentance and judgement. This is not the only place in the gospels where an unfruitful tree is given short shrift: John the Baptist declared that 'the axe is lying at the root of the trees' (Luke 3:9), and Jesus warned that his Father 'removes every branch in me that bears no fruit' (John 15:2). Here, however, Luke balances the warning of God's judgement with the promise of God's mercy. Judgement will come, but the parable also recognises that we are works in progress and that, during our lives, God gives us every opportunity to work with, rather than against, God.

The parable invites us to identify with the unfruitful tree that is shown mercy. We are given time, but in that time we are expected to be serious about seeking an ever-deepening relationship with God. This is not about achieving in human terms; it is more about cultivating a willing openness to being led by God, who will help us to bear fruit in ways we may not be able to see or imagine.

Yes, we need to be patient with ourselves; but we also need to take care that our patience doesn't become complacency. We have been blessed with the gift of life; but we also know that life is fragile and can be ended at any moment.

The unfruitful fig tree is granted an extra year to make amends; how would each of us choose to live now, if we knew we had only one more year?

BARBARA MOSSE

Garden of betrayal

While he was still speaking, Judas, one of the twelve, arrived; with him was a large crown with swords and clubs, from the chief priests and the elders of the people... At once [Judas] came up to Jesus and said, 'Greetings, Rabbi!' and kissed him. Jesus said to him, 'Friend, do what you are here to do.' Then they came and laid hands on Jesus and arrested him... At that hour Jesus said to the crowds, 'Have you come out with swords and clubs to arrest me as though I were a bandit? Day after day I sat in the temple teaching, and you did not arrest me. But all this has taken place, so that the scriptures of the prophets may be fulfilled.' Then all the disciples deserted him and fled.

We return to the garden of Gethsemane for a second visit, but this time from a very different perspective. Some time has passed; Jesus has poured out his agony over his coming ordeal to his Father and chided his friends for their persistent sleepiness and inability to watch with him. Now the traitorous disciple Judas Iscariot bursts on to the scene intent on Jesus' arrest, with a mob of priests and people in support. This event is recorded in all four gospels, and the accounts have an almost filmic quality: vivid words make it easy to imagine the threatening faces of the mob, illuminated by the flickering flames of the torches, with the darkness of the night making visible the darkness in Judas' heart.

The garden as the scene of this highly charged meeting is significant. Gethsemane has been a place Jesus frequently retreated to (Luke 22:39). Judas knew where to find him, and the fact that he brought a totally disproportionate crowd with him suggests he didn't expect to find Jesus alone. This place of fellowship has now been despoiled by Judas' treachery and the disciples' desertion.

But we are all complicit here. Rather than pointing the finger and saying, 'I'd never behave like that!', are we prepared to let the disciples' behaviour here put under scrutiny those times we have let other people down?

'The Pharisee... was praying thus, "God, I thank you that I am not like other people"' (Luke 18:11).

BARBARA MOSSE

Why are you weeping?

But Mary stood weeping outside the tomb… She turned round and saw Jesus standing there, but she did not know that it was Jesus. Jesus said to her, 'Woman, why are you weeping? For whom are you looking?' Supposing him to be the gardener, she said to him, 'Sir, if you have carried him away, tell me where you have laid him, and I will take him away.' Jesus said to her, 'Mary!' She turned and said to him in Hebrew, 'Rabbouni!' (which means Teacher). Jesus said to her, 'Do not hold on to me, because I have not yet ascended to the Father. But go to my brothers…' Mary Magdalene went and announced to the disciples, 'I have seen the Lord'; and she told them that he had said these things to her.

Today's garden is the site of Jesus' tomb. It's the place of one of those very strange post-resurrection appearances when the people who were closest to Jesus during his public ministry initially failed to recognise him (see also Luke 24:13–35 and John 21:4–14). Here, the grief-stricken Mary responds to the questions of a man she takes to be the gardener, before eventually recognising him as Jesus when he calls her by name.

To begin with, the atmosphere in this garden is bleak and seemingly hopeless. After all, what can be more final than death? It seems that the reality of Jesus' death and Mary's overwhelming grief combine to prevent her from seeing and accepting the evidence in front of her eyes: that it is indeed Jesus standing before her.

This lack of recognition may seem strange to us, but is it *that* strange? In how many of the various 'garden' situations in our lives do we fail to see and recognise the Christ who has promised never to leave us (Matthew 28:20)? Many of us will have experienced bereavement and understand the grief Mary was experiencing. But lack of recognition can also happen in other difficult or painful situations, when it may feel that God is absent. Perhaps our view of God is too small; at such times we need to pray that God will both enlarge our vision and deepen our trust.

Be thou my vision, O Lord of my heart.

BARBARA MOSSE

Paradise regained

'Let anyone who has an ear listen to what the Spirit is saying to the churches. To everyone who conquers, I will give permission to eat from the tree of life that is in the paradise of God...' Then the angel showed me the river of the water of life, bright as crystal, flowing from the throne of God and of the Lamb through the middle of the street of the city. On either side of the river is the tree of life with its twelve kinds of fruit, producing its fruit each month; and the leaves of the tree are for the healing of the nations.

We have come full circle. There is no explicit mention of a garden here; indeed, the setting is a city. But the reference to paradise makes the connection with the garden of Eden quite clear. The river flowing out of Eden (Genesis 2:10) becomes the river flowing through the city; the tree of life in the midst of the garden (Genesis 2:9) is here the tree of life bursting with fruit and healing foliage. And the tree's healing properties extend way beyond the boundaries of the original garden; they are for 'the healing of the nations' (22:2).

When we consider the sad and desperate state of our world, we may wonder how such a healing is possible. The gap between our present experience and this vision seems unbridgeable. But, thank God, we are not required to *understand* how such a healing can come about; only to believe and trust that, in God's good time, it will. There is a hymn by W.Y. Fullerton (1857–1932), sung to the tune 'Londonderry Air', which captures this hope and longing perfectly. The first four lines of each verse begin 'I cannot tell', expressing our anguish at the pain and injustice in the world. But the second group of four lines respond with a resounding 'But this I know', affirming our belief in God's vision for our future.

'God is working his purpose out, as year succeeds to year.
God is working his purpose out, and the time is drawing near;
Nearer and nearer draws the time, the time that shall surely be
When the earth shall be full of the glory of God, as the waters cover
the sea' (A.C. Ainger, 1894).

BARBARA MOSSE

Ezekiel

The book of Ezekiel is one of the more challenging books we will encounter, containing as it does 'the promise of endless smiting', in the words of one of my children. Certainly it does contain some very lurid passages. First it is the turn of the people of Israel to be told in great detail what will happen to them as a punishment for their continual disobedience of God and their fracturing of their covenant with him. Next, the book moves on to describe the disastrous levels of punishment that will thunder down upon those nations that oppose Israel, to such a degree that we wonder what has become of the loving God who wants only the best for each one of us.

However, these messages of anger and vengeance are not the primary theme of the book. What becomes gradually clearer as the chapters unroll is the purpose that God has for all the people of the world – that they should know his voice – and the particular role that Israel has – ensuring God's voice is heard. This role is not merely a community responsibility but an individual one as well; spreading the message of God's power and the glory of his kingdom is one that all people are tasked with, both then and now.

This teaching is combined with the visions of that glory and the promises and hope that are offered by the prophet to a world desperate to hear words of a future containing freedom, justice, love and hope. And, of course, the book of Ezekiel includes those two golden passages – the promise that each one of us will have our 'hearts of stone' turned into 'hearts of flesh' with the advent of the Spirit, and the picture of the 'valley of dry bones' brought to life by that same Spirit. Written at a turning point in Israel's history, these pictures of hope can speak to us just as they did to the children of Israel, far from home, refugees in a strange land.

These 14 reflections will, I hope, enable us to come to an understanding of the nature and relevance of Ezekiel's words for us today.

SALLY WELCH

Who was Ezekiel?

In the thirtieth year, in the fourth month, on the fifth day of the month, as I was among the exiles by the river Chebar, the heavens were opened, and I saw visions of God. On the fifth day of the month (it was the fifth year of the exile of King Jehoiachin), the word of the Lord came to the priest Ezekiel son of Buzi, in the land of the Chaldeans by the river Chebar; and the hand of the Lord was on him there.

Who was Ezekiel? Much of what we know comes from his own writings. The Hebrew name means 'God strengthens', and it was certainly an appropriate name when we consider the circumstances in which he worked. Initially living in Jerusalem, Ezekiel, like his father before him, was a priest in the temple there, carrying out the prescribed tasks and duties of that most privileged of groups. Serving in the holiest of sites, the place where God had chosen to reside among his people in the land that he had given them, Ezekiel must have felt the honour of such a position. Then the worst disaster happens – Judah is invaded by King Nebuchadnezzar and its inhabitants are sent into exile in Babylon. In one swift action, Ezekiel loses everything he has and is forced to begin a new life in a foreign country.

Although a fortunate few of us will have spent our whole lives in settled happiness, most people will experience disaster of one type or another in the course of their lives. Perhaps the events will not be as dramatic as occupation by a foreign power and subsequent exile, but traumatic occurrences, such as job loss, financial upset, serious illness or death, have the power to overthrow our lives completely, so that we lose all sense of stability and security. At those times it is easy to lose sight of God or to find our trust in him frayed or even vanished. But it is while standing with his fellow exiles by a strange river in an unfamiliar land that Ezekiel has a vision of God that sustains him in his difficulties.

In the darkest times, a single light burns brightly.

SALLY WELCH

Visions of glory

As I looked, a stormy wind came out of the north: a great cloud with brightness around it and fire flashing forth continually, and in the middle of the fire, something like gleaming amber. In the middle of it was something like four living creatures. This was their appearance: they were of human form... As for the appearance of their faces: the four had the face of a human being, the face of a lion on the right side, the face of an ox on the left side, and the face of an eagle; such were their faces... Like the bow in a cloud on a rainy day, such was the appearance of the splendour all round. This was the appearance of the likeness of the glory of the Lord.

The very first thing that Ezekiel shares with us is a vision of God's glory. For us, this vision seems strange and unfamiliar, but perhaps this just serves to heighten the comparison between our everyday, predictable world and the greatness of its creator. Too often we try to domesticate God; to predict or even dictate what he will do; to give him human emotions and reactions; to reduce him to a likeness of ourselves, in fact, rather than the other way round – seeing in ourselves glimpses of the almighty, all-powerful ruler of all things.

So, at times when we do not understand why events are unfolding as they are, when situations seem unfair and cruel, we can draw hope from the fabulous visions of Ezekiel as they remind us who is in control. And in the middle of the picture, we find the faces of the human being, the ox, the lion and the eagle, images that were taken up as early as the second century AD to represent the four gospel writers. The most common view is that of fourth-century Jerome, who argued that the gospel of Matthew, beginning with a genealogy, is represented by a man; Mark's prophet roared in the desert like a lion; Luke's gospel favoured the ox, as it began with a temple sacrifice; and John's 'Word' flew up towards the heavens like the eagle. Thus, at the strangest point, we find the familiar.

Lord God, help me remember your glory.

SALLY WELCH

Exile

The spirit lifted me up and bore me away; I went in bitterness in the heat of my spirit, the hand of the Lord being strong upon me. I came to the exiles at Tel-abib, who lived by the river Chebar. And I sat there among them, stunned, for seven days. At the end of seven days, the word of the Lord came to me: Mortal, I have made you a sentinel for the house of Israel; whenever you hear a word from my mouth, you shall give them warning from me.

Many of us have been stunned by the pictures of exiles and refugees that daily assault us from all parts of the world. The utter misery and hopelessness of people who have lived many days in terrible fear, hiding from enemies, trying to help the wounded despite a lack of medical resources, and witnessing death and destruction, is written on their faces. That trauma of this level should then be followed by a terrifying escape, only for the journey to end in the mud and chaos of a refugee camp, where hope seems absent and life is cheap, compounds the agony.

Seemingly helpless in the face of so much suffering, we wonder what we can do to help and how such things can be allowed to happen. Where is the compassionate and loving God in this, we ask? It is no comfort to discover that situations such as these have been happening for centuries, and that Ezekiel too experienced the mayhem and the chaos of exile, finding the emotion of bitterness all too easily.

From these depths the prophet goes on to speak, reminding Israel that it has brought its own destruction upon itself, through sin and disobedience, wilfully turning from the way of the Lord. So too must we bear responsibility for the plight of the helpless, as we allow our corporate greed and lust for power to overcome our common humanity, our love for the easy life to block our generosity and obligation to share.

Forgive us, Lord, for our selfish and greedy actions;
show us how we can change our ways.

SALLY WELCH

The rivers of Babylon

By the rivers of Babylon we sat and wept when we remembered Zion. There on the poplars we hung our harps... How can we sing the songs of the Lord while in a foreign land?

For years, the country of Judah had been caught between the powers of Egypt and Babylon. Finally, in 589BC, King Nebuchadnezzar of Babylon invaded the country and sent many of its people into exile. He then set about laying siege to Jerusalem. This very act struck terror into the hearts of the exiles. The city of Jerusalem was more than just the capital of a country; for the children of Israel, it was the beating heart of God's promise to them. God's covenant of care, his personal involvement with his children, was embodied in the stone buildings of the temple; it was where God himself dwelt, and as such it had long been thought to be inviolable. God's people could not believe that God would abandon it – and yet he did. In 587, Jerusalem fell, its buildings destroyed, its temple ransacked. The unimaginable had happened. If God's house on earth had gone, where then was God?

When the people or situations that we have depended upon are overturned or fail, we may find ourselves in a 'strange land', one whose landscape is unfamiliar and which we cannot call home. Then we may indeed sit by the rivers of our own personal Babylon, with the singers of Psalm 137, and weep as we remember happier times in Zion.

We are not forbidden to mourn or to lament at the misfortunes that have befallen us. We do not have to be silent as we sit in the sun-burned valley, surrounded by the dry bones of our hopes and dreams. We can call out amid the wreckage of our lives and ask for help to sing the songs of the Lord in a foreign land. This is what the children of Israel do, and the words of Ezekiel are their answer.

Teach me, Lord, how to sing your song when I am in a strange land, and help me to teach others how to find their voices also.

SALLY WELCH

Ezekiel's mission

He said: 'Son of man, I am sending you to the Israelites, to a rebellious nation that has rebelled against me; they and their ancestors have been in revolt against me to this very day. The people to whom I am sending you are obstinate and stubborn. Say to them, "This is what the Sovereign Lord says." And whether they listen or fail to listen – for they are a rebellious people – they will know that a prophet has been among them.'

Driven into exile with his people, Ezekiel must first have been at a huge loss as to what to do. Previously his days would have been full of the ritual of his work at the temple in Jerusalem. He would have enjoyed significant status and respect – he may have been a well-known figure and perhaps enjoyed some comfort and prosperity. Now all that has been taken from him, and he is simply an exile living with his fellow exiles.

But God has other plans for him – he must speak out to the children of Israel on God's behalf. Ezekiel has been chosen to reprimand his people, to tell them the unpleasant truth that what has happened to them is a result of their own sin, and that further punishment awaits. Ezekiel isn't even given a guarantee of success at this difficult task – for it doesn't matter 'whether they listen or fail to listen'. But they do need to know that 'a prophet has been among them' (v. 5), for that is the first stage in their rescue and redemption.

Sudden downturns in our personal fortunes or happiness can have a devastating effect upon us. Loss of job through redundancy or retirement can mean losing our position in our community, even our self-respect. The loss of a partner or loved one may mean we must renegotiate how others view us and how to live in a new context. But through all the changes, our Christian witness must remain constant. We must strive to live our lives in a way that reveals the gospel to those around us, so that they will know a prophet has been among them.

'He came as a witness to testify concerning that light,
so that through him all might believe' (John 1:7).

SALLY WELCH

Thorns and scorpions

'And you, son of man, do not be afraid of them or their words. Do not be afraid, though briers and thorns are all around you and you live among scorpions. Do not be afraid of what they say or be terrified by them, though they are a rebellious people. You must speak my words to them, whether they listen or fail to listen, for they are rebellious.'

What wonderfully comforting words – 'Do not be afraid, though briars and thorns are all around you and you live among scorpions' (v. 6)! Possibly the briars, thorns and scorpions were real for Ezekiel; more likely they were a wonderful metaphor for the pain caused by the words, deliberate or simply careless, of others. How often the casual comment or carefully positioned barb can make us cry out in mental pain! How many times have we felt belittled or mocked by others, or hurt by a remark made in jest or anger?

But how many times has this been because of our faith? Are we enthusiastic sharers of the gospel, eager to tell others about Christ's saving action and God's redeeming love? Or are we rather quiet Christians, content simply to go to church or prayer group, sharing in community tasks perhaps but unwilling actually to share our faith with those around us? At times, simply living as Christians in our community is enough – our actions witness to those who see how we treat others with grace and kindness, help those who are in need and serve others before ourselves. But sometimes we need to speak out, to explain the reasons behind our actions, to tell what motivates us and why Christ has changed our lives.

Sometimes this speaking will not be well received, and we will be scratched by thorny rejections and stung by scorpion words. Yet still we must speak, because there will be others who are waiting to hear about the one who loves us for who we are, frail and faulty, the one who wants to help us become fully human, the one who died so that we might not.

'We have a gospel to proclaim
Good news for all throughout the earth;
The gospel of a Saviour's name:
We sing his glory, tell his worth'
(Edward Burns, 1815).

SALLY WELCH

Eat this book

And he said to me, 'Son of man, eat what is before you, eat this scroll; then go and speak to the people of Israel.' So I opened my mouth, and he gave me the scroll to eat. Then he said to me, 'Son of man, eat this scroll I am giving you and fill your stomach with it.' So I ate it, and it tasted as sweet as honey in my mouth.

Like most churches, ours holds a service on Good Friday for children and families, where we explore the Easter story in accessible ways. One of my favourite ways to do this is through different types of food. Obviously, we finish with hot cross buns; their symbolism is familiar and well-loved, as is the sharing of bread and grape juice as we reflect on the last supper. But we also include pretzels, whose curved shape reminds us of the crossed arms of the prayerful monks who first made this snack; bitter herbs to remember the garden of Gethsemane (parsley dipped in salt water); and pieces of apple as we recall the first sin of Adam and Eve. Eating provides another way of absorbing, remembering, entering the story.

Ezekiel, too, is charged with 'eating' the words of God as a way of taking them completely into himself. His study of the word of God is so intense that it becomes part of his body; he is at one with God's purpose for him and God's message for his people. And the twofold message of this passage reminds us not only of the vital importance of studying the scripture, of engaging deeply with its message, but also of the gift of the Word himself, who lived among us, was betrayed by us and was sacrificed for us so that we might live. This is the Word we eat at Holy Communion, which tastes as sweet as honey as it provides sustenance so that we might live.

'While they were eating, Jesus took bread, and when he had given thanks, he broke it and gave it to his disciples, saying, "Take and eat; this is my body"' (Matthew 26:26).

SALLY WELCH

Watchmen

At the end of seven days the word of the Lord came to me: 'Son of man, I have made you a watchman for the people of Israel; so hear the word I speak and give them warning from me. When I say to a wicked person, "You will surely die," and you do not warn them or speak out to dissuade them from their evil ways in order to save their life, that wicked person will die for their sin, and I will hold you accountable for their blood. But if you do warn the wicked person and they do not turn from their wickedness or from their evil ways, they will die for their sin; but you will have saved yourself.'

One of the reasons that the book of the prophet Ezekiel is so difficult to read is that much of the content involves God warning his people of the consequences of their actions. 'You have been more unruly than the nations around you and have not followed my decrees or kept my laws,' God says through Ezekiel (5:7). Therefore, terrible things will happen: 'in your midst parents will eat their children, and children will eat their parents' (5:10). As if this wasn't enough, Ezekiel then prophesies disastrous events for the countries surrounding Judah for their part in its invasion: 'They will be desolate among desolate lands, and their cities will lie among ruined cities' (30:7).

Appalling phrases pour out of Ezekiel's mouth, until the words are almost impossible to hear. Why such anger? Because God has spared the people of Israel again and again. Despite their disobedience, he withheld his hand (20:22), until it was clear that they needed a sharper voice. Ezekiel's role is to be that voice.

How difficult it is to speak out when we witness wrongdoing! How much easier to keep quiet. But God tells Ezekiel that if he does not speak, he will be 'accountable for their blood' (v. 18). So we have a duty to act when we see injustice or hatred, prejudice or violence.

We are the 'watchmen' of our communities; but we must be on watch against ourselves as well, that we do not also fail.

SALLY WELCH

A royal priesthood

Then Moses went up to God, and the Lord called to him from the mountain and said, 'This is what you are to say to the descendants of Jacob and what you are to tell the people of Israel: "You yourselves have seen what I did to Egypt, and how I carried you on eagles' wings and brought you to myself. Now if you obey me fully and keep my covenant, then out of all nations you will be my treasured possession. Although the whole earth is mine, you will be for me a kingdom of priests and a holy nation." These are the words you are to speak to the Israelites.'

The Israelites fled Egypt three months previously and have just entered the Sinai desert. Moses meets God on the mountain and receives new instructions for his people. From now on, they will be a 'a kingdom of priests and a holy nation' (v. 6). What does this mean? It means that the whole people of Israel are bound in covenant to perform the tasks of priests: offering prayers for the world, making sacrifices on behalf of others and teaching nations about God and his works. 'For the lips of a priest ought to preserve knowledge, because he is the messenger of the Lord Almighty and people seek instruction from his mouth' (Malachi 2:7).

Ezekiel is a priest and called to be a prophet. But that role is not reserved simply for those set aside as priests. As children of God, we too are a 'royal priesthood, a holy nation'; we too are bidden to 'declare the praises of him who called you out of darkness into his wonderful light' (1 Peter 2:9). We may not feel called to the role of prophet, but we can share our experience of God's saving grace in our lives and in the lives of those around us. We can work to make our communities prayerful and obedient to the word of God, serving God through our service to others and our worship and praise.

'Take my voice, and let me sing
Always, only, for my King;
Take my lips, and let them be
Filled with messages from Thee'
(Frances Ridley Havergal, 1836–79).

SALLY WELCH

Falling into sin

Then he said to them, 'Defile the temple and fill the courts with the slain. Go!' So they went out and began killing throughout the city. While they were killing and I was left alone, I fell face down, crying out, 'Alas, Sovereign Lord! Are you going to destroy the entire remnant of Israel in this outpouring of your wrath on Jerusalem?' He answered me, 'The sin of the people of Israel and Judah is exceedingly great; the land is full of bloodshed and the city is full of injustice. They say, "The Lord has forsaken the land; the Lord does not see." So I will not look on them with pity or spare them, but I will bring down on their own heads what they have done.'

God is showing the prophet a terrible glimpse of the future – the city of Jerusalem destroyed and the temple defiled. Again and again, God affirms that this punishment is due to the failing of his people: 'I will bring down on their own heads what they have done' (v. 10). This does not make the punishment less harsh but does help us to understand it better. God himself is being scorned by other nations; not only is Israel breaking the covenant, but other countries too are denied the opportunity of hearing God's voice.

Some of the terrible things that happen to us are completely outside our control; others are not. Sometimes we bring disaster upon ourselves, by our failure to act with loving compassion, by our negligence or carelessness, 'through our own deliberate fault', as the *Book of Common Prayer* confession reminds us. In a challenging and sometimes frightening world, we must keep our hearts steady and fixed on God, not only to avoid falling into sin but also to find a resource and help when we do run into danger, whether through our own fault or not.

'Grant that this day we fall into no sin, neither run into any kind of danger, but that all our doings may be ordered by thy governance, to do always that is righteous in thy sight' (The Collect for Grace from a service of Morning Prayer, Book of Common Prayer, 1662).

SALLY WELCH

Building Jerusalem

'Therefore say: "This is what the Sovereign Lord says: although I sent them far away among the nations and scattered them among the countries, yet for a little while I have been a sanctuary for them in the countries where they have gone." Therefore say: "This is what the Sovereign Lord says: I will gather you from the nations and bring you back from the countries where you have been scattered, and I will give you back the land of Israel again."'

We have seen how the prophet Ezekiel spoke to the people of Israel about their responsibility for the disasters that had come upon them. He also spoke of the retribution God would work upon the nations that had played a part in this destruction and of the terrible justice that would be wreaked upon them. Now, however, comes the time for hope. People cannot live under fear for a long time without becoming paralysed by it. People cannot be constantly reminded of their offences without being given a way forward, or they will remain miserably trapped forever.

So God shares with Ezekiel two promises. First, he reminds the prophet that even while in exile, God has been there for him and for all the Israelites – 'a sanctuary for them in the countries where they have gone' (v. 16). Then he promises that, in time, they will return from exile and the land of Israel will be theirs once more.

In our times of exile, when we are led into a strange and unfamiliar land, where we must navigate through new landscapes, we can remember God's presence and find sanctuary there. We can hold on to the promise that it is in Christ that we will find the new Jerusalem and that we have already entered our promised land; we simply have to look around us.

'I will not cease from mental fight,
Nor shall my sword sleep in my hand:
Till we have built Jerusalem,
In England's green and pleasant land.'
Beneath his hymn 'Jerusalem', William Blake wrote,
'Would to God that all the Lord's people were Prophets' (Numbers 11:29).
How can we build Jerusalem where we are today?

SALLY WELCH

105

Heart of stone, heart of flesh

'For I will take you out of the nations; I will gather you from all the countries and bring you back into your own land. I will sprinkle clean water on you, and you will be clean; I will cleanse you from all your impurities and from all your idols. I will give you a new heart and put a new spirit in you; I will remove from you your heart of stone and give you a heart of flesh. And I will put my Spirit in you and move you to follow my decrees and be careful to keep my laws. Then you will live in the land I gave your ancestors; you will be my people, and I will be your God.'

The promises in this passage make it one of my favourite parts of the Old Testament. Once again, God calls Ezekiel to relay a message of hope to his people. He will bring them back to their own land and allow them to begin again. He will take away the burden of sin and pain and allow them to live and breathe freely again. Obedience to his covenant will become easier, since the Spirit of God will live within them, and they will be his people once more.

What beautiful words, and how they echo down the centuries, as we see them made new and fresh in the life and works of Christ! Through the waters of baptism, we are given the opportunity to be washed clean of all our sins. Through Christ's death and resurrection, this opportunity is held out to us again and again as we repent and are forgiven by his grace. The Spirit, who descended upon the disciples at Pentecost, lives and breathes within us, transforming our stony hearts into living, loving instruments of God's love as 'God lives in us and his love is perfected in us' (1 John 4:12, NRSV). As we eat and drink at the Lord's table, we become dwellers in his Word made flesh.

'Hearts of stone, relent, relent!
Break, by Jesus' cross subdued…
with all my sins I'll part:
Saviour, take my broken heart'
(Charles Wesley, 1707–88).

SALLY WELCH

'Dem dry bones'

[The Lord] said to me, 'Prophesy to these bones and say to them, "Dry bones, hear the word of the Lord! This is what the Sovereign Lord says to these bones: I will make breath enter you, and you will come to life. I will attach tendons to you and make flesh come upon you and cover you with skin; I will put breath in you, and you will come to life. Then you will know that I am the Lord."'

And finally we reach the most famous passage from Ezekiel – God leads Ezekiel out into a valley covered with 'a great many bones… bones that were very dry' (37:2). God asks Ezekiel if he thinks the bones can live, to which Ezekiel replies that only God knows the answer. God's response is in this glorious promise. Ezekiel knows that the people of Israel feel cut off from every hope. But the future of Israel does not end in the valley. The place of dry bones does not remain the site of despair and death but is instead the ideal setting for gaining new visions of God.

The one thing that can change this landscape of brokenness is the breath of God. The God of the impossible can transform the bones of death into an army of life. The breath of God creates a new future. The scattered bones of the valley are gathered together when Ezekiel speaks words of hope to them. But they remain lifeless until the breath of God, the Spirit of God, is breathed into them.

So too must we seek the breath of God, to breathe life into our apparently lifeless situations. We may not find him where we used to find him, and so we must look in new places. But one of the disciplines of faith is hope. One of the tasks is the determined inbreathing of new life, of new ways of thinking and believing, seeking and looking. And always we remember that we do not carry out these tasks alone.

'Ezekiel connected dem dry bones,
Ezekiel connected dem dry bones,
Ezekiel in the Valley of Dry Bones,
Now hear the word of the Lord'
(James Weldon Johnson, 1871–1938).

SALLY WELCH

'I am with you always'

'This is the land you are to allot as an inheritance to the tribes of Israel, and these will be their portions,' declares the Sovereign Lord... 'The distance all around will be 18,000 cubits. And the name of the city from that time on will be: The Lord is there.'

The book of Ezekiel ends with a magnificent recitation of the land and the temple that will be allotted to the children of Israel on their return to the promised land. It is highly detailed, perhaps as a way of helping those in exile build a mental picture of their future; something tangible to hold on to during the undoubtedly challenging times to come. This picture is drawn upon at the end of the New Testament, when John writes of his vision of the 'Holy City, the new Jerusalem' (Revelation 21:2). Both authors wrote to a community under pressure; both understood the need for hope and to keep alive the promise of a time when '"he will wipe every tear from their eyes. There will be no more death" or mourning or crying or pain, for the old order of things has passed away' (Revelation 21:4).

The first turning point in Israel's history came with the exodus from Egypt, a people led by Moses exploring what it meant to be the children of God. Here lies another turning point – the exile of a disobedient people as a stark reminder of the dangers of a broken covenant. Distraught and suffering, they are offered a vision of a future where they can dwell once again in the house of the Lord, filled with the breath of his life-giving Spirit, dry bones given flesh once more.

The final turning point is the Christ event, when the Word of the promise becomes flesh and all nations on earth are offered redemption. Salvation history has reached its pinnacle – our task now is to live as a redeemed people, bringing the news of Christ's love to all nations and rejoicing in his presence here among us.

'And surely I am with you always, to the very end of the age'
(Matthew 28:20).

SALLY WELCH

Holy Week and Easter in Matthew

While I was writing these reflections in mid-November, the global and national news was unremittingly bad and many people were feeling a sense of hopelessness. We were heading into winter and the weather wasn't helping. One day I went for a walk through the fields near my home. I picked my way along a muddy lane, casting a glance at the distant sky where dark clouds were gathering. But then my gaze was caught by a scene much closer at hand. Beyond the track stretched a field, recently ploughed and now already greening with the first shoots of a fresh crop. Suddenly the sunlight broke through a gap in the clouds and lit up the whole field, making every tender new shoot gleam. It was a moment of joy amid the November gloom.

Such a moment catches the very spirit of Eastertide, but more specifically it also reflects a pattern of contrasting darkness and light, fear and love, threat and promise, death and life, that defines Matthew's account of the events of Passiontide and Easter. Throughout these final chapters of Matthew's gospel, we are confronted again and again by contrasting situations and values, and challenged to reflect on what these mean in our own lives.

The journey to the cross, and beyond, begins with 'Hosanna!' but rapidly changes to 'Crucify!' It leads on through sinister rumblings of conspiracy on the one hand and outpourings of love on the other. We hear empty promises of loyalty, which will soon be broken, and we hear Jesus' promise that nothing shall extinguish the light of divine love. We participate in the dark emptiness of the tomb, and we discover that it is also the place where new life is gestating. We face the reality of lies and deception in our lives and our world, and at the same time we see the power of unshakeable truth. We witness the kiss of betrayal and the embrace of unconditional love, authentic and inauthentic authority, blind destructive obedience and clear-sighted thoughtful compliance.

And finally, holding all contradictions and tensions in his hands and his heart, the risen Christ gives us his blessing. Through dark and shining days, times of despair and rejoicing, his promise never fails: 'I am with you always.'

MARGARET SILF

From 'Hosanna!' to 'Crucify!'

The disciples went and did as Jesus had directed them; they brought the donkey and the colt, and put their cloaks on them, and he sat on them. A very large crowd spread their cloaks on the road, and others cut branches from the trees and spread them on the road. The crowds that went ahead of him and that followed were shouting: 'Hosanna to the Son of David! Blessed is the one who comes in the name of the Lord! Hosanna in the highest heaven!'

Today we celebrate the triumphal entry of Jesus into Jerusalem. Immediately, however, we notice how far from our understanding of 'triumphal' this event really is. There is a quiet obedience in the way Jesus' friends carry out his instructions and in his own choice to ride into Jerusalem on a donkey. This is a very far cry from the frequently ostentatious conduct of many of today's celebrities. Indeed, the 21st-century attitude to 'celebrity' would surely have been anathema to Jesus.

And then the cry goes up – 'Hosanna… Hosanna in the highest heaven!' (v. 9). Had we been present, would we not also have been shouting our 'Hosanna'? Yet many of those who cry 'Hosanna' will, in just a few short days, be calling 'Crucify!'

How rapidly 'Hosanna!' becomes 'Crucify!' How readily and enthusiastically we support those who are riding the crest of the wave – the winning football team, the popular speaker, the fashionable opinion. And how promptly we drop them like hot potatoes when they displease or disappoint us, attract opposition or simply go out of fashion.

Everywhere in today's world we see this roller coaster of alternating adulation and vilification in action. A hard but necessary lesson in this is that if something is inherently wrong, it does not become right just because it appears to succeed; and vice versa.

The gospel draws us back to first principles: the life and teaching of Jesus are fundamentally good and true. That goodness and truth do not depend on our 'Hosanna', nor can they be shaken by our 'Crucify'.

May we stop and think before we cry 'Hosanna!'
And may we kneel and pray before we call 'Crucify!'

MARGARET SILF

Whispers of conspiracy

When Jesus had finished saying all these things, he said to his disciples, 'You know that after two days the Passover is coming, and the Son of Man will be handed over to be crucified.' Then the chief priests and the elders of the people gathered in the palace of the high priest, who was called Caiaphas, and they conspired to arrest Jesus by stealth and kill him. But they said, 'Not during the festival, or there may be a riot among the people.'

We are living in an age that seems to relish conspiracy theories. We are also uncomfortably familiar with the nature and the language of violence. Jesus is fully aware of the deadly rumblings among those who are conspiring to destroy him, and he warns his friends accordingly. In the light of his clarity of mind and spirit, the cloak-and-dagger discussions of the chief priests and elders would appear ridiculous, if it were not for the severity of the situation.

Their plans display all the hallmarks of the sinister. They gather secretly and plot to seize their victim by stealth. They are driven by fear. They are afraid of the power of Jesus to transform society, afraid of the coming of a very different kind of kingdom that will challenge their own little empires. But the elimination of Jesus stirs another deep-seated fear: the people might revolt if they carry out their plans during the festival.

Such machinations are very familiar to our world today, but now, as then, the reaction of the people is a factor to be considered. Yet we, the people, usually feel helpless to resist these sinister movements in our world or even to realise that they are happening. Today's reading may be helpful. The language of secrecy almost always indicates sinister intentions. What is whispered in secret is usually contrary to the values of the kingdom. But openness and honesty begin in our own hearts. Where do we detect tendencies to secrecy or stirrings of destructive fear? Can we bring what we find into the light of God's healing?

May we have the courage to look into our own hearts and ask God to show us any secret whispers we may find there, and free us from the fears that feed them.

MARGARET SILF

111

Outpourings of love

Now while Jesus was at Bethany in the house of Simon the leper, a woman came to him with an alabaster jar of very costly ointment, and she poured it on his head as he sat at the table. But when the disciples saw it, they were angry and said, 'Why this waste? For this ointment could have been sold for a large sum, and the money given to the poor.' But Jesus, aware of this, said to them, 'Why do you trouble the woman?... By pouring this ointment on my body she has prepared me for burial.'

While yesterday's reading took us into the sinister shadows of conspiracy, today we meet Jesus in a place of generosity and love. We move from hostile whispering to an open outpouring of devotion.

Conspiracy conceals itself in silence and secrecy, creeping into the darkest corner. This woman's love for Jesus breaks out of all constraints and taboos and quite simply overflows. But such an outpouring also provokes criticism. The disciples are angry, ostensibly because the value of the ointment could have been spent to help the poor, but perhaps also with a touch of jealousy when the love expressed by another person threatens to eclipse their own. Jesus seems to hint at this himself, as he reminds them of just what this anointing means to him. Conspiracy cannot break his spirit, but love, and love alone, can prepare him for all that lies ahead.

So where do we find ourselves in this scene? Yesterday we caught a glimpse of the darker corners of our hearts where fear and suspicion lurk. Can we today identify with the love and goodness that also dwell within us, longing to overflow? How do we express our love, for God and for each other? Are we ever critical of others when their love seems to flow more readily than our own? But love is not a competition. Each of us has his or her own ways of expressing what is closest to our hearts. What does this mean to you personally?

May we have the courage to respond to the promptings of love in our hearts and not be afraid to let it overflow into the lives of others.

MARGARET SILF

Promises, firm or frail

Then Jesus said to them, 'You will all become deserters because of me... But after I am raised up, I will go ahead of you to Galilee.' Peter said to him, 'Though all become deserters because of you, I will never desert you.' Jesus said to him, 'Truly I tell you, this very night, before the cock crows, you will deny me three times.' Peter said to him, 'Even though I must die with you, I will not deny you.' And so said all the disciples.

Promises, promises. We have heard far too many of them, and made plenty of our own, and frequently seen them dissolve into thin air. A colleague of mine had a fridge magnet on her desk which read: 'When the going gets tough, the tough get going.' Perhaps this catches something of the spirit of today's reading, as tough, impulsive Peter is challenged by the truth that only Jesus knows.

First, we hear Jesus' stark warning, followed by his breathtaking promise. What a terrible thing to hear, when the man you believe will change the world tells you that you will desert him in his hour of need. Peter's indignant protest is understandable, but his promise to stay alongside Jesus, even unto death, is a hollow one, as Jesus knows. He underlines the emptiness of Peter's promise in the detail of the denial that will follow before cockcrow.

But just listen to Jesus' promise. When everything indicates that this is the end of the line for himself, his vision and his friends, he promises them that he will transcend death itself and go ahead of them, back to Galilee. Jesus is speaking out of the deep eternal truth in his heart, which neither fear nor falsehood can diminish. Peter is merely articulating what he wants to be true but is quite unable, in his own strength, to fulfil.

We can, however, be reassured that whenever we make a promise from the deepest, truest centre of our being, the grace to live true to what we have promised will be given, and the Holy Spirit will go ahead of us in all our ways.

May every promise we make be rooted in the source of all truth.

MARGARET SILF

Sleeping partners?

And going a little farther, [Jesus] threw himself on the ground and prayed, 'My Father, if it is possible, let this cup pass from me; yet not what I want but what you want.' Then he came to the disciples and found them sleeping; and he said to Peter, 'So, could you not stay awake with me one hour? Stay awake and pray that you may not come into the time of trial; the spirit indeed is willing, but the flesh is weak.'

The frailty of Peter's promise of solidarity with Jesus is quickly exposed in Gethsemane. While Jesus wrestles with the horrors of his impending torture and death, his friends are asleep. Their exhaustion is completely understandable. Would we have been able to 'stay awake'? Many people today are so inwardly fatigued by the turmoil and conflict all around us that they can no longer watch the TV news. It is so much easier to close our eyes to the things we can't bear to see. To stay awake forces us to participate in the pain of the world and of each other. Few of us can handle that.

Jesus understands our frailty. He knows that our spirits truly desire to stand in solidarity with him and with the world's pain, but our 'flesh is weak' (v. 41). We are human, and his own humanity reaches out to touch ours.

One sleepless night I remembered this scene in Gethsemane. Just for a moment it felt as though my unwanted wakefulness had become a blessing – an opportunity for solidarity with those whose nights are fractured by pain, sorrow or fear, and, in them, also with Jesus in his suffering.

We are human. We need to sleep, and there is a limit to how much pain we can bear. This is why we are asked to share the burden of sorrow in whatever ways we can. Next time you are unable to sleep, you might just go to your window and see whether any other lights are burning in your street. To be, for a few moments, at one with your suffering neighbour is a real response to Jesus' request to 'stay awake'.

If we stay awake with Jesus through the dark, we will also see the dawn with him.

MARGARET SILF

Abdication

Pilate said to them, 'Then what should I do with Jesus who is called the Messiah?' All of them said, 'Let him be crucified!'... So when Pilate saw that he could do nothing, but rather that a riot was beginning, he took some water and washed his hands before the crowd, saying, 'I am innocent of this man's blood; see to it yourselves.' Then the people as a whole answered, 'His blood be on us and on our children!' So he released Barabbas for them; and after flogging Jesus, he handed him over to be crucified.

Peter, with his extravagant promises, impetuous actions and fine words, is not one to hold back. Pilate has a very different personality. While Peter faces trouble head-on, at least until raw fear drives him into denial on the morning of Good Friday, Pilate knows how to walk the line of least resistance.

Once during a retreat, I was trying to enter imaginatively into the events of Holy Week. It was probably this scene, with Pilate, that most disturbed me, because I recognised something of myself in him. I find confrontation very difficult, and I too am very ready to 'wash my hands' of anything that requires active resistance. I had to admit to myself, during that retreat, that I can be something of an appeaser – eager to please, or at least placate, everyone, and in doing so risk abdicating moral responsibility.

Pilate very simply transfers the responsibility for Jesus' death to the crowd. Without any idea of the significance or the consequences of what they are doing, they demand Jesus' blood, and Pilate 'handed him over'.

What does this mean for us today? Was it right for Pilate to set aside his own authority and listen instead entirely to the voice of the people? What about our personal decisions? How ready are we to abdicate our own responsibility for a decision entrusted to us, and hand it over to others? In today's world, where the lines of individual and collective responsibility are often blurred, these questions remain very relevant to both our public and private lives.

May we have the grace to recognise the responsibilities we must own,
and those we need to share.

MARGARET SILF

Entombed

When it was evening, there came a rich man from Arimathea, named Joseph, who was also a disciple of Jesus. He went to Pilate and asked for the body of Jesus; then Pilate ordered it to be given to him. So Joseph took the body and wrapped it in a clean linen cloth and laid it in his own new tomb, which he had hewn in the rock. He then rolled a great stone to the door of the tomb and went away. Mary Magdalene and the other Mary were there, sitting opposite the tomb.

The most important Jesus events seem to take place in dark, empty places. He begins his human journey in a maiden's womb. He completes it in a stranger's tomb. These are the spaces of transformation. They are far from empty. They are brimming with life-potential, just as a seed, still closed up in its husk, holds the still-unimaginable future potential, not just of one plant but of an entire species of plant.

Too often Easter Saturday is bypassed, treated as a vacant space between the agony of Good Friday and the joy of Easter Sunday – or, in more secular terms, between the hot cross buns and the Easter eggs. It's much harder to identify with the apparent nothingness of Saturday, but empty space is the place where God is growing a kingdom beyond anything we can ask or imagine.

Surely, then, our own inner emptiness can also be a place where the seeds of transformation might germinate. As you journey through Easter Saturday, allow yourself to join Jesus in the tomb. Invite God to anoint all that feels dead and hopeless within you. Surrender your heart-space to the void as the stone is rolled into place, enclosing you in darkness and silence. Imagine your soul as a tiny seed, planted in the darkness of the tomb. In the fullness of eternity that seed will release the unique person God has always been dreaming into being in your life. It will birth the completeness of everything you truly are.

Joseph of Arimathea showed great courage in asking for permission to bury Jesus. May we share in that courage by daring to rest in the tomb of transformation, awaiting the fulfilment of the divine promise.

MARGARET SILF

Sunrise of a new dawn

After the sabbath, as the first day of the week was dawning, Mary Magdalene and the other Mary went to see the tomb. And suddenly there was a great earthquake; for an angel of the Lord, descending from heaven, came and rolled back the stone and sat on it. His appearance was like lightning, and his clothing white as snow. For fear of him the guards shook and became like dead men.

Ireland is home to several ancient burial mounds, constructed four millennia ago, that are carefully aligned with earth and sky to allow the first light of dawn on, variously, the winter or summer solstice to strike through a narrow slot in the stonework and flood the inner chamber with light. There is a similar chamber at Maeshowe on Orkney in northern Scotland.

We know the earth was shaken and the veil of the temple rent in two, as Jesus surrendered his life on the cross, but today's earthquake heralds dawn not darkness. The tearing of the veil of the temple is rather like the narrow slot in the stonework of these ancient monuments – it allows a new dawn to penetrate our darkness, flooding human life with the light of new beginnings.

This Easter earthquake is accompanied by an angel, who rolls back the stone and releases the fullness of life from the entombment of death. The very appearance of the angel is like lightning – another symbol of cosmic upheaval – and his snow-white clothing reflects the light that now streams forth from the place of death and destruction.

The guards are shaken to the core, paralysed by the sheer force of the energy that has been released. We are promised no less. We have shared, in our own way, in Jesus' passion and death. We have spent time in the tomb of our own deepest despair. Today is the day of awakening, when all that is dead inside us is flooded with the dawn-light of resurrection. It is a timeless moment, a record of a past event, a present reality and a promise of all that shall be.

As we walk the paths of our earthly lives, stumbling through our history into God's mystery, may the light of this new dawn illuminate our every step.

MARGARET SILF

Easter Day   117

Silent witness

The high priest stood up and said, 'Have you no answer? What is it that they testify against you?' But Jesus was silent. Then the high priest said to him, 'I put you under oath before the living God, tell us if you are the Messiah, the Son of God.' Jesus said to him, 'You have said so. But I tell you, From now on you will see the Son of Man seated at the right hand of Power and coming on the clouds of heaven.'

In this second week of our reflections, we begin to see how the light of resurrection reveals the shadow side of human hearts and societies. Today's reading takes us back to Jesus' appearance before the high priest, where he reveals that the events of Easter will change everything and that his ways and God's ways are not our ways or the high priest's ways.

When challenged with false allegations, Jesus is silent. Placed under oath and asked whether he is the Messiah, he replies simply that these are his accuser's words, not his own. He then goes on to speak of what is to come. Even as he stands on the brink of a dreadful death, he gives us a glimpse of what lies beyond.

Jesus' silent witness makes space for a greater truth, eclipsing the lies of false witness as the heat of the midday sun withers the weeds. The light of his testimony exposes the nature of power. The high priest's human power carries no weight with the one who will be seated at the right hand of true power. Human authority imposes power over us, forcing compliance. Divine authority empowers us from within, inviting us to become the people we are created to be.

We notice too that Jesus describes himself as the Son of Man, not only emphasising his humanity rather than his divinity, but also reminding us of our own humanity and its potential to share in the risen life of the Christ.

The Son of Man opens a door into new ways of being fully alive – a door where we thought there was only a solid wall. May we have the courage to follow his invitation to grow beyond death into the fullness of life.

MARGARET SILF

Looking for Jesus

At that hour Jesus said to the crowds, 'Have you come out with swords and clubs to arrest me as though I were a bandit? Day after day I sat in the temple teaching, and you did not arrest me'… But the angel said to the women, 'Do not be afraid; I know that you are looking for Jesus who was crucified. He is not here; for he has been raised, as he said. Come, see the place where he lay. Then go quickly and tell his disciples, "He has been raised from the dead, and indeed he is going ahead of you to Galilee; there you will see him." This is my message for you.'

In Jerusalem there is a garden incorporating a tomb that may have been the one in which Jesus was laid to rest. This garden tomb is in stark contrast to the Church of the Holy Sepulchre, officially considered to be Jesus' burial place. The Holy Sepulchre is a place of endless streams of tourists and pilgrims, and not without a degree of conflict between its various guardians. The garden tomb is a place of tranquillity and peace, making no extravagant claims, but humbly offering itself as a place of calm reflection.

The most memorable feature of the garden tomb, however, is a simple inscription above the entrance, reading, 'He is not here. He is risen.' I'll never forget how I felt when I first read those words. Perhaps in some small way I was hearing the message the angel gave to the women who were searching for Jesus 2,000 years ago.

Love doesn't hide in the shadows. It can't be pursued by force or imprisoned by human chains. Love is often found where we never thought to look for it, and it takes us completely by surprise. Love does not dwell with death, but always goes ahead of us, leading us gently towards new life. What can we learn from the events of today's reading about our own search for love?

May our eyes be opened to discover the love of God in unexpected places and the risen Christ in the midst of life. Wherever we are, he goes ahead of us, leading us to where we need to be.

MARGARET SILF

119

Two greetings

The betrayer had given them a sign, saying, 'The one I kiss is the man; arrest him.' At once he came up to Jesus and said, 'Greetings, Rabbi!' and kissed him... [The women] left the tomb quickly with fear and great joy, and ran to tell his disciples. Suddenly Jesus met them and said, 'Greetings!' And they came to him, took hold of his feet, and worshipped him. Then Jesus said to them, 'Do not be afraid; go and tell my brothers to go to Galilee; there they will see me.'

Our greetings can be completely casual – a hurried 'good morning' to a neighbour or a passing stranger – or very profound, as when we meet someone who means a great deal to us. They are, however, or so we might think, rarely a matter of life or death, as in our readings today. But is this really so?

There is something appalling about the kiss of betrayal. To hand a friend over to death with a kiss touches the lowest depths of human nature. By contrast, the joyous greeting of the women, overwhelmed by the reality of resurrection, transcends all normal boundaries of human rejoicing.

We mostly hover somewhere between these two extremes. We cannot imagine betraying a friend with a kiss, but we are more than capable of betraying a confidence with a false word or dishonouring a friendship by a malicious comment. We may fall short of the ecstatic joy of the women at the empty tomb, but we know the delight of greeting a loved one returning from a long absence or from the brink of serious illness.

Today's readings remind us that greetings really matter. A single thoughtless or deliberately malicious remark or comment, especially comments made anonymously online, can destroy something in the spirit of a fellow human being. Words can be like poisoned arrows. They can kill. On the other hand, even a casual greeting can convey warmth and sincerity and help another person feel more alive, more respected, more loved. Words can be carriers of hope, confidence, compassion, life. They can be arrows of divine grace.

In everything we say, and to everyone we greet, may we be messengers of life, peace and love.

MARGARET SILF

Truth in a web of falsehood

Now when the centurion and those with him, who were keeping watch over Jesus, saw the earthquake and what took place, they were terrified and said, 'Truly this man was God's Son!'... While they were going, some of the guard went into the city and told the chief priests everything that had happened. After the priests had assembled with the elders, they devised a plan to give a large sum of money to the soldiers, telling them, 'You must say, "His disciples came by night and stole him away while we were asleep."'

Two of the most disturbing features of our times are the blurring of the line between truth and falsehood and the widespread erosion of trust in many of our institutions. Falsehood and deception are no newcomers to the human scene. Today's reading reveals two contrasting incidents. One describes a meeting to plan the invention of 'fake news'; the other records a moment of truth.

The politics that flourish on fake news seem not to have changed much over time. The chief priests and elders have a problem: Jesus' resurrection was not part of their plan. The 'troublemaker' they thought they had eliminated has left the tomb. How are they going to cover up this turn of events and conceal the truth from the people? It doesn't take them long to come up with an alternative story. Those in the know must then be persuaded, through bribery, to spread the lies, and an uncomfortable truth is suppressed by a fabrication that is maintained by deception and corruption.

How different is the moment when the centurion and his companions, who had witnessed the actual events surrounding Jesus' death, make their simple, powerful declaration of truth! Shaken to the core by all that has happened, they have the courage to look truth in the eye and acknowledge what they see.

Deep in our hearts we know those moments of truth. Let us not allow them to be obscured by the webs of falsehood so often woven around us.

The real name for 'fake news' and 'alternative facts' is lies. There is no alternative name for truth. Truth stands in its own light and speaks for itself. May we have the grace to recognise the difference.

MARGARET SILF

Only obeying orders

Suddenly, one of those with Jesus put his hand on his sword, drew it, and struck the slave of the high priest, cutting off his ear. Then Jesus said to him, 'Put your sword back into its place; for all who take the sword will perish by the sword'... [The chief priests said,] 'If this comes to the governor's ears, we will satisfy him and keep you out of trouble.' So [the guards] took the money and did as they were directed. And this story is still told among the Jews to this day.

Ever since Adam and Eve, we have tried to excuse our behaviour by blaming someone else. One of the most popular excuses is the argument that we were only obeying orders.

Today we see two very different examples of 'obeying orders'. In the first, Jesus himself gives the order, to prevent further aggression against his pursuers, with the warning that violence will always lead to more violence. This is a serious order, issued in love and wisdom. It is obeyed, because Jesus' friends respect him and the reason for his intervention.

By contrast the high priests' order arises from the fear of the consequences if the governor hears of Jesus' disappearance from the grave. And so, bribed and coerced, the guards do as they are told, in an attempt to pass a false story down through history. If we could ask them now why they took this course of action, they would surely say they were just obeying orders.

Life can pitch us into difficult situations involving serious moral dilemmas. Sometimes we are tempted to take the easy way out: do as we are told and then absolve ourselves on the grounds that the greater sin lies with the one who gave the orders. Sometimes the fear that leads to blind obedience is extreme, for example in a brutal dictatorship. We are ultimately responsible for our own choices and must leave to God the judgement of those who gave the orders, but divine love reads our hearts, and is merciful.

May we have the grace to obey the voice of truth and love in our hearts, and the courage to resist the demands that come from those with sinister motives.

MARGARET SILF

A question of authority

Now Jesus stood before the governor; and the governor asked him, 'Are you the King of the Jews?' Jesus said, 'You say so.' But when he was accused by the chief priests and elders, he did not answer... so that the governor was greatly amazed... Now the eleven disciples went to Galilee, to the mountain to which Jesus had directed them. When they saw him, they worshipped him; but some doubted. And Jesus came and said to them, 'All authority in heaven and on earth has been given to me.'

I like to imagine the look on the governor's face when Jesus responds to his question by turning it right back with his words, 'You say so', and then reacting to the chief priests' and elders' accusation with an eloquent silence. This is not the response one would expect of someone on trial for his life. Jesus doesn't try to defend or explain himself. Perhaps, the governor may be thinking, he is simply scornful of his interrogators, considering their questions unworthy of a response. Perhaps he is in a different plane of reality in which these normal responses are irrelevant. Whatever the reason, Jesus is quietly refusing to acknowledge the authority of these men, which he knows is not grounded in God, but is a reflection of human power systems. This possibility has never occurred to the governor before. No wonder he is greatly amazed.

The second part of the reading provides deeper insight into the question of authority. Jesus has transcended all that human authority could inflict upon him, and he now meets his friends in Galilee as he had promised. Their reactions range from doubt to wonder, and Jesus reassures them by explaining the source of his own authority. Unlike the self-appointed power of the governor and elders, Jesus' authority has been given to him by the author of all being.

We are constantly subjected to the demands of human 'authorities', and in some situations we exercise authority ourselves. Remembering that the only truly valid authority is a gift from God may help us discern how to respond to, and how to exercise, human authority in our world.

In every situation may we ask ourselves, 'Who is the true author of this authority?'

MARGARET SILF

With you always

They led [Jesus] away to crucify him. As they went out, they came upon a man from Cyrene named Simon; they compelled this man to carry his cross... [Jesus said,] 'Go therefore and make disciples of all nations, baptising them in the name of the Father and of the Son and of the Holy Spirit, and teaching them to obey everything that I have commanded you. And remember, I am with you always, to the end of the age.'

'I am with you always' is a commitment that only love can make and only total unconditional love can fulfil. Our own such commitments all too easily falter and fail, but today we hear of two very different ways of providing this kind of companionship. The first is forced by circumstances, as Simon of Cyrene is compelled to accompany Jesus and carry his cross. This is far from being a choice made from love, but nevertheless Simon is, from that moment on, the closest companion to Jesus in his suffering and death.

This incident has been the inspiration of a person I knew, whose husband had suffered life-changing injuries in a catastrophic accident only a short time after their wedding. Circumstances had overturned both their lives, and she found herself, a young woman with a life ahead of her, now exclusively committed to caring full-time for her husband. Her prayers had taken her to the accounts of Jesus' last days, and she identified strongly with Simon, forced to carry another's cross, contrary to everything he had planned or hoped for. She discovered for herself that this unwished-for commitment was a call to come closer both to Jesus and to her husband. She found peace, alongside Simon of Cyrene.

In the second part of the reading Jesus is sending out his friends into what will prove to be a hostile world. This commission is laid upon us today, no less than upon them, and it feels overwhelming. Jesus knows this and makes his love-promise, to us just as to them: 'I am with you always', whatever life brings.

Look back, and remember: he was with you. Stand still, and realise: he is with you. Walk forward, and trust: he will be with you always.

MARGARET SILF

Some favourite prayers

Some prayers stick in my mind; others grab me as vital for the moment; some qualify for consideration as favourites on both counts. But what ultimately qualifies a prayer for me so that I can label it as an all-time favourite?

It doesn't have to be in contemporary language, although that sometimes helps. It doesn't need to be couched in beautiful prose or poetry, though I certainly appreciate those qualities. What it must do is be very much like 'speaking in tongues'; it must say to God exactly what I am feeling, deep in my heart, but which my limited mind is unable to find the right words to express. I hope some of these prayers will be like that for you as they are for me.

When it comes to my everyday prayer routine, I find it necessary to have a prayer schedule of some sort to keep me on track, and my present discipline goes like this – Sunday: thanksgiving for all of God's goodness; Monday: my extended family; Tuesday: the church (local, national and universal); Wednesday: mostly listening to hear what God might have to say to me; Thursday: urgent and pressing needs, the sick and suffering known to me; Friday: my friends; Saturday: oppressed, persecuted and refugee Christians. Some of the prayers I have chosen will reflect this pattern.

'What about missions?' you might say. 'What about the poor and homeless?' Yes, of course there are some obvious gaps. This is why all Christians are called to pray. Perhaps you are the one to fill in one of those big gaps in my prayer schedule.

Being a Kiwi, I will naturally draw most of my favourite prayers from *A New Zealand Prayer Book – He Karakia Mihinare o Aotearoa*, which is a real treasure store of prayer. It provides a choice of three collects for each Sunday as well as a host of prayers for all occasions.

I am indebted to the General Secretary of the Church in New Zealand, Polynesia and Aotearoa for permission to use material from *A New Zealand Prayer Book – He Karakia Mihinare o Aotearoa* for the reflections on 21–24, 26 and 30 April and to the Barnabas Fund for permission to use their prayer on 27 April.

PAUL GRAVELLE

Blessing homes

Zacchaeus… welcomed [Jesus] with great joy. All the people who saw it started grumbling, 'This man has gone as a guest to the home of a sinner!' Zacchaeus stood up and said to the Lord, 'Listen, sir! I will give half my belongings to the poor, and if I have cheated anyone, I will pay back four times as much.' Jesus said to him, 'Salvation has come to this house today, for this man, also, is a descendant of Abraham. The Son of Man came to seek and to save the lost.'

Everyone knew that this home was an evil place before Jesus came, and they could certainly sense the difference that his presence brought about. It would seem that Zacchaeus was anxious to change his dishonest business ethics but didn't know how to set about it. Still uncertain, he had climbed a tree to get a glimpse of Jesus as he passed by, but Jesus discerned not just his presence but also his hidden longing and forced the issue dramatically by inviting himself into Zacchaeus' home. The very thought of Jesus' close presence in this way appeared to have been the tipping point in the taxman's conversion, and this must have totally dumbfounded the critics in the crowd.

I am regularly called upon to officiate at the blessing of a home where there has been some evil manifestation or violent event, and there is a need to banish evil and invite the Spirit of Jesus to take up permanent residence in its place. The liturgy that we use is modelled on one from the Church of South India, and this has been entirely effective in bringing peace to the affected homes. Our house blessings always conclude with this prayer.

Lord God Almighty, Father of every family, against whom no door can be shut, enter into the homes of our land we pray. Make them places where your love is known and understood by each person. By your dear Son, born in a stable, move our hearts to hear the cry of the homeless and to convert all sordid, bitter and hopeless dwellings into households where you are truly welcomed, through Jesus Christ our Lord. Amen

PAUL GRAVELLE

Prayer for unity in Christ

'I am the vine, and you are the branches. Those who remain in me, and I in them, will bear much fruit; for you can do nothing without me. Those who do not remain in me are thrown out like a branch and dry up; such branches are gathered up and thrown into the fire, where they are burned... My Father's glory is shown by your bearing much fruit; and in this way you become my disciples.'

These words of Jesus could take up a week of reflections, but I want us to look particularly at the amazing statement with which the passage begins. Here in New Zealand, everyone is familiar with what a grapevine looks like. Viticulturists train the branches of each plant out along wire frameworks so that they reach out way beyond the root systems. Jesus does not say, 'I am the root,' or, 'I am the main stem,' but, 'I am the vine' – the entire plant. Then he says, 'You are the branches.' Jesus is saying that each of us is actually an integral part of himself! Do you find that hard to grasp? I certainly do.

The enemy would love to see us tear ourselves apart and thereby away from the vine. He has often tried to do that in the past but has had only small success. In the present climate, where the church as a whole, as well as separate denominations and congregations, is beset by differing interpretations of scripture on a number of matters, same-sex relationships in particular, unity in Christ takes on a pressing importance for many.

It seems to me that God, in his wisdom, allows us some leeway in our understanding of his truth. He gives us grace to worship differently, to belong to different churches and even to behave in somewhat different ways. If we are able to live with that, we can remain in the vine, united to Christ, and bear much fruit.

Creator God, you have made us not in one mould, but in many:
so deepen our unity in Christ that we may rejoice in our diversity
and work together to spread the good news of your kingdom.
Hear this prayer for your love's sake. Amen

PAUL GRAVELLE

Praying to receive the Holy Spirit

It was late that Sunday evening, and the disciples were gathered together behind locked doors, because they were afraid of the Jewish authorities. Then Jesus came and stood among them. 'Peace be with you,' he said. After saying this, he showed them his hands and his side. The disciples were filled with joy at seeing the Lord. Jesus said to them again, 'Peace be with you. As the Father sent me, so I send you.' Then he breathed on them and said, 'Receive the Holy Spirit.'

There is a big difference between giving and receiving. When I was four years old, I was given a pair of school socks for Christmas. I threw them back at the giver. I wanted toy soldiers. I certainly didn't receive that gift! The believers didn't receive the Holy Spirit immediately, but at Pentecost everyone knew that they had received.

There are differing opinions about when God gives his Holy Spirit – at our baptism, conversion or some other time. But there is no doubt about our receiving, because whenever we receive the Holy Spirit, we are set free. We can experience freedom to pray in new ways and to serve others as we have never done before. In my experience, we may be freed from fear and prejudice too.

When Jesus told the disciples that he was sending them in the same way that the Father sent him, he meant that literally. They were to be given the same Spirit that he had received at his baptism. They would be equipped for ministry and service in exactly the same way that he had been. As Peter shouted out in his great sermon at Pentecost, this promise is for everyone. 'God's promise,' he proclaimed, 'was made to you and your children, and to all who are far away – all whom the Lord our God calls to himself' (Acts 2:39). Thank you, Lord, that the promise is for each one of us!

Living God, eternal Holy Spirit, let your bright intoxicating energy which fired those first disciples fall on us to turn the world again. Set us free to hear your word to us; set us free to serve you. This we ask through Christ our Redeemer. Amen

PAUL GRAVELLE

Prayer for the healing of the sick

The Lord appointed seventy-two others and sent them two by two ahead of him to every town and place where he was about to go. He told them, 'The harvest is plentiful, but the workers are few. Ask the Lord of the harvest, therefore, to send out workers into his harvest field... When you enter a town... Heal those there who are ill and tell them, "The kingdom of God has come near to you"'... The seventy-two returned with joy and said, 'Lord, even the demons submit to us in your name.'

I can remember a time when we never prayed for the sick. It was thought that miracles and healings had ceased and that it was wrong to ask God for supernatural happenings. As a result, no one was healed. Nowadays we seem to have changed our minds. We do pray for people who are ill, and some of them are wonderfully healed. These 72 were sent out in the same way as the twelve, but these were unnamed followers of Jesus, ordinary people like you and me. They are included in the gospel story to show us that all of Jesus' followers are equipped by his Holy Spirit to demonstrate his healing power and by doing so to proclaim the kingdom of God.

Jesus himself proclaimed the kingdom of God by his preaching and by his ministry of healing and other miracles. In this way he convinced many more than these 72! In your church there are those who have gifts of preaching, but what about the ministry of healing and other miraculous activities? As Jesus said, 'The harvest is plentiful, but the workers are few. Ask the Lord of the harvest, therefore, to send out workers into his harvest field.' But, be prepared. He might well say, 'How about you?'

This prayer is one of the collects for the third Sunday after Epiphany in the *New Zealand Prayer Book*.

Jesus, our Redeemer, give us your power to reveal and proclaim the good news, so that wherever we may go, the sick may be healed, lepers embraced, and the dead and dying given new life. Praise to you our God, you answer prayer. Amen

PAUL GRAVELLE

Praying to be ready for his coming

There is no need to write to you, friends, about the times and occasions when these things will happen. For you yourselves know very well that the Day of the Lord will come as a thief comes at night. When people say, 'Everything is quiet and safe,' then suddenly destruction will hit them! It will come as suddenly as the pains that come upon a woman in labour, and people will not escape. But you, friends, are not in the darkness, and the Day should not take you by surprise like a thief.

The Jewish people had always looked forward to 'the day of the Lord', when everything would change: swords would be turned into ploughshares, sorrow and mourning would disappear and every hope would be fulfilled. Christians can now add the promise of the angels at Jesus' ascension, that this climactic day will be the one when Christ himself returns.

The prayer below is one of our collects for Advent Sunday. It seems to me, however, that after that first Sunday we spend the rest of the Advent season looking back towards Christmas instead of looking forward to Jesus' return. Look at the pictures on the average Advent calendar and you'll see what I mean.

Advent is the season of the year when Christians should be concentrating on the fact that Jesus Christ is coming back to reign on earth and, whether we are still here or somewhere in eternity at the time, this will be the day of resurrection and all the redeemed will be there to meet with him.

Paul's words to the Christians in Thessalonica and the prayer below remind us that, as citizens of the kingdom of God, we are expected to be not only aware of, but also actively engaged in paving the way for, the coming of King Jesus. How can you best work to prepare the way for Christ's return?

God of hope, when Christ your Son appears may he not find us asleep
or idle, but active in his service and ready, who lives and reigns with you
and the Holy Spirit, one God forever. Amen

PAUL GRAVELLE

Praying for our country

You people who live in Jerusalem will not weep any more. The Lord is compassionate, and when you cry to him for help, he will answer you. The Lord will make you go through hard times, but he himself will be there to teach you, and you will not have to search for him any more. If you wander off the road to the right or the left, you will hear his voice behind you saying, 'Here is the road. Follow it.' You will take your idols plated with silver and… gold, and will throw them away.

Isaiah assures the people that God is always ready to forgive and to guide them, if they will only turn towards him instead of towards false objects of worship.

Every land has its false idols, and Christians need to be constantly in prayer for those in authority and for the people of their own country. In New Zealand and Australia, today is Anzac Day, the equivalent of the UK's Armistice Day, when we remember the fallen of the Australia and New Zealand Army Corps from World War I and others of our two nations who have died in the service of their country. Here in Auckland, there will be a dawn service at the Cenotaph, and each town and suburb will have a similar service at its own war memorial.

I was once asked to conduct such a service and posed the question to the assembled ex-servicemen and their families, 'What would our fallen comrades think if they were to return now and see the depraved state into which we have allowed our country to fall?' It was no surprise that I was not asked back the following year!

I thank God that New Zealand's national anthem is a prayer asking that God will indeed defend us against the evils of worshipping false idols, evils that threaten any nation.

God of nations at thy feet, in the bonds of love we meet,
Hear our voices, we entreat, God defend our free land…
From dissension, envy, hate, and corruption guard our state,
Make our country good and great, God defend New Zealand. Amen

PAUL GRAVELLE

Holy Communion

Jesus said to them, 'I am telling you the truth: if you do not eat the flesh of the Son of Man and drink his blood, you will not have life in yourselves. Those who eat my flesh and drink my blood have eternal life, and I will raise them to life on the last day. For my flesh is the real food; my blood is the real drink. Those who eat my flesh and drink my blood live in me, and I live in them... Those who eat this bread will live forever.'

No wonder the synagogue congregation at Capernaum were confused and angry when they heard this from Jesus. The very idea of drinking blood was totally repugnant to every Jew. Ever since the Reformation and for somewhat different reasons, Christians have also become confused over the meaning of these words of Jesus. Sadly, they have even been angry enough to become seriously divided over them. Some of us will venerate the bread and wine, understanding the words in a literal sense. Others of us will see the Communion elements as aids to meditation on the significance of Jesus' death. There will be many shades of understanding in between these extremes.

No matter how we interpret Jesus' words, all of us who are obedient to his command at the last supper to 'do this in memory of me' (Luke 22:19) will speak of our action as Communion. Communion means 'sharing of thoughts' or 'fellowship', and when we share in Communion we are sharing thoughts and having fellowship with Jesus himself.

When I kneel at the altar rail, I am in communion with Jesus. I meet with him there; I am endeavouring to share his thoughts; I may even hear his voice speaking into my mind. At Communion we are in communion with someone we can know intimately. Today's prayer is a section from one of our great thanksgiving prayers in New Zealand.

Send your Holy Spirit that these gifts of bread and wine, which we receive, may be to us the body and blood of Christ, and that we, filled with the Spirit's grace and power, may be renewed for the service of your kingdom.

PAUL GRAVELLE

Prayer for refugees and the oppressed

An angel of the Lord appeared in a dream to Joseph and said, 'Herod will be looking for the child in order to kill him. So get up, take the child and his mother and escape to Egypt, and stay there until I tell you to leave.' Joseph got up, took the child and his mother, and left during the night for Egypt, where he stayed until Herod died. This was done to make come true what the Lord had said through the prophet, 'I called my Son out of Egypt.'

The holy family became refugees for a time, so we can see that escaping to another country to avoid threats from opponents of our faith is not a new situation. It is still happening to Christians today, in Sudan, Syria, India and many other countries. A good proportion of the refugees in our world today are our brothers and sisters in Christ. Christians are losing their homes through war; others are in prison or have lost their jobs; some are even experiencing martyrdom at the hands of terrorists. It is hard for us to imagine what opposition or persecution of this kind is like. I hope most of us can go to work, worship at our church and sleep safely at night without fear of threats from governments, religious authorities or even our neighbours.

A number of Christian relief agencies are hard at work to bring help to refugees and others who are suffering hardship through persecution. They are all worthy of our prayers and help in whatever way we can.

One such organisation is Barnabas Fund. Today's prayer, 'Prayer for the Suffering Church', is from a Barnabas Fund bookmark, which I keep in my BRF notes.

God of all compassion, visit your suffering people. In the time of their troubles, let them not be dismayed. In their oppression, let them not be destroyed. In their anxiety, let them not lose hope. In their alienation and wandering, be their identity and their home. In their fragility and brokenness, be their strength and treasure. Let your light shine upon them and reveal the glory of your eternal Son, in whose name we pray. Amen

PAUL GRAVELLE

Asking God to speak to us clearly

The Lord called Samuel a third time; he got up, went to Eli, and said, 'You called me, and here I am.' Then Eli realised that it was the Lord who was calling the boy, so he said to him, 'Go back to bed; and if he calls you again, say, "Speak, Lord, your servant is listening."' So Samuel went back to bed. The Lord came and stood there, and called as he had before, 'Samuel! Samuel!' Samuel answered, 'Speak; your servant is listening.'

God speaks in a number of ways, and anyone can listen to his voice if their ears are tuned in to what he is saying. Like Samuel, we need to check that it really is God who is speaking to us; in other words, to ask for confirmation. God will always say the same thing in another way if we ask him.

The most obvious way God speaks is through the Bible itself. After all, it is God's word, right there in print and, with *New Daylight*, we are in the right place to hear!

One Sunday, the sermon I was listening to seemed utterly irrelevant. I was almost asleep when I heard some words in my mind: 'You will do better than this for me.' God was calling me! I have now been privileged to serve in ministry for over 40 years. Be ready for words to pop into your mind unexpectedly!

One of the common situations in which we need to hear God's voice is when faced with important choices. It is helpful to ask God to close the gate to any wrong path. This is not so much God speaking as taking action, but it has the same effect.

Sometimes, too, God will speak through the words of someone else: a preacher, a friend or even a complete stranger. While someone might say something to you that brings help, comfort or encouragement from God, you could well find yourself being God's mouthpiece for someone else.

Today's prayer is the opening verse of a hymn by Frances Ridley Havergal (1836–79).

Lord, speak to me, that I may speak in living echoes of thy tone;
as thou hast sought, so let me seek thy erring children lost and lone.

PAUL GRAVELLE

Praying through a great project

Our enemies thought we would not see them or know what was happening until they were already upon us, killing us and putting an end to our work… From then on half of my men worked and half stood guard, wearing coats of armour and armed with spears, shields, and bows. And our leaders gave their full support to the people who were rebuilding the wall. Even those who carried building materials worked with one hand and kept a weapon in the other.

Nehemiah had set himself a massive project: to rebuild the ruined walls of Jerusalem in the face of serious opposition. One of the ways in which he brought the work to a successful conclusion was by arming the workers against surprise attack. Nehemiah's builders were warriors as well. They overcame the difficulties they faced, and the walls were completed.

Any project undertaken for the sake of the kingdom of God is unlikely to go smoothly and may not even succeed without the active support of dedicated prayer warriors. The parish where I work is geographically the largest in our city and the population is growing at an astonishing rate. The parish church is small, but the congregation is increasing and designs for a fine new building have been approved. A good proportion of the money needed has been raised, but outside organisations must now be approached for the balance. Right from the outset, 'prayer warriors' have been at work, every step in the planning process being supported by much prayer.

This prayer, attributed to Sir Francis Drake, is a declaration of his conviction about big projects. He doesn't mention the need for supporting prayer, but I feel that the implication is certainly there. Our redeemer, Jesus Christ, through whom Sir Francis offers his prayer, was often going off to pray about the task the Father had set before him.

Lord God, when thou givest to thy servants to endeavour any great matter, grant us also to know that it is not the beginning, but the continuing of the same, until it be thoroughly finished, that yieldeth the true glory; through him who, for the finishing of thy work, laid down his life for us, our Redeemer, Jesus Christ. Amen

PAUL GRAVELLE

Peace at the last

Wolves and sheep will live together in peace, and leopards will lie down with young goats. Calves and lion cubs will feed together, and little children will take care of them. Cows and bears will eat together, and their calves and cubs will lie down in peace. Lions will eat straw as cattle do. Even a baby will not be harmed if it plays near a poisonous snake. On Zion, God's sacred hill, there will be nothing harmful or evil. The land will be as full of knowledge of the Lord as the seas are full of water.

In this prophecy of the peaceful kingdom, Isaiah gives us a series of examples of what life here will be like when Jesus returns and is reigning as king. The Bible contains a number of prophecies concerning peace among humans, echoes of which are found in unlikely places – in the musical *Les Misérables*, for example, 'The Epilogue' speaks of men walking peacefully behind the plough and putting away the sword (Isaiah 2:4). While conditions like this are hard for us to imagine, most of us long for peace between nations, between political and social factions, between racial and neighbourhood groups and within families – in fact, wherever there is discord, danger and hostility.

The last prayer in this series is a beautiful one, which I use in most funeral services. It contrasts the turmoil of everyday life with a request for a peaceful passing from this one to the next. I like to think that it goes way beyond that point to our promised post-resurrection life. Then, when Jesus is king over all the earth, all of the promises in the Bible concerning that time will become reality. Then we will truly be in a position to experience the 'peace which is far beyond human understanding' (Philippians 4:7). Don't forget that this life is a rehearsal for the real performance.

Support us, Lord, all the day long of this troubled life, until the shadows lengthen, and the evening comes, the busy world is hushed, the fever of life is over, and our work is done. Then, Lord, in your mercy, give us safe lodging, a holy rest and peace at the last. This we ask through Christ our Saviour. Amen

PAUL GRAVELLE

Reading *New Daylight* in a group

SALLY WELCH

I am aware that although some of you cherish the moments of quiet during the day which enable you to read and reflect on the passages we offer you in *New Daylight*, other readers prefer to study in small groups, to enable conversation and discussion and the sharing of insights. With this in mind, here are some ideas for discussion starters within a study group. Some of the questions are generic and can be applied to any set of contributions within this issue; others are specific to certain sets of readings. I hope they generate some interesting reflections and conversations!

General discussion starters

These can be used for any study series within this issue. Remember there are no right or wrong answers – these questions are simply to enable a group to engage in conversation.

- What do you think the main idea or theme of the author in this series? Do you think they succeeded in communicating this to you, or were you more interested in the side issues?

- Have you had any experience of the issues that are raised in the study? How have they affected your life?

- What evidence does the author use to support their ideas? Do they use personal observations and experience, facts, quotations from other authorities? Which appeals to you most?

- Does the author make a 'call to action'? Is that call realistic and achievable? Do you think their ideas will work in the secular world?

- Can you identify specific passages that struck you personally – as interesting, profound, difficult to understand or illuminating?

- Did you learn something new reading this series? Will you think differently about some things, and if so, what are they?

Questions for specific series

What hath God wrought! (Murdo Macdonald)

Murdo suggests that our walk with God can be 'assisted and augmented using technology'. In what ways has your walk with God been helped by technology? How has it been hindered? Murdo writes about the chronic fuel poverty suffered by some people – how might you change your attitude to using the resources of the planet? How might this help others?

Gardens (Barbara Mosse)

How big a part do gardens or green spaces play in your life? How would your life be without them? Do you agree with Martin Luther that 'God writes the gospel not in the Bible alone but on trees and flowers and clouds and stars'? What sort of gospel message might this be? How might your worshipping community engage more with creation?

Ezekiel (Sally Welch)

Are there areas in your life which seem like 'dry bones' at the moment? Why are they dry – through your own actions or through circumstances beyond your control? Is there a way in which you can 'breathe life' into the situation? Remember God's promise: 'I will put breath in you, and you will come to life. Then you will know that I am the Lord' (Ezekiel 37:6, NIV).

New author interview: Murdo Macdonald

You have titled your reflections 'What hath God wrought!' Why?

The quote is from Numbers 23:23. In 1844, these words were the first official Morse code message transmitted in the USA. As scientists, we have the enormous privilege of pushing the boundaries of what we know. But with that knowledge comes additional responsibility. Part of the role of Christians who are actively engaged in science and technology is to respond to the call to be 'salt and light' in seeking to encourage responsible use and applications of technological developments.

You trained as a molecular biologist. How did you end up working with The Leprosy Mission in Nepal?

Following my PhD my career path was fairly routine, with appointments in university and research institutions. However, I always felt called to use my skills in a more explicitly Christian context, so when the opportunity to serve as head of The Leprosy Mission research labs in Nepal presented itself, I jumped at the chance.

What was it like living in Nepal?

Although Rachel and I went out to Nepal separately, we were already good friends, and, following an engagement in Nepal, we came back to the UK briefly in 2001 to get married. The first few years of our marriage we lived in the Leprosy Mission hospital in Nepal. Our older two children were born in Kathmandu; the birth of our youngest after we moved back to Edinburgh certainly served to reinforce how good the UK NHS is in comparison to the best healthcare Nepal has to offer! Nepal is a beautiful country, though not without its problems and frustrations; the people are also lovely, but the culture is very different from what we are used to, with things like personal space, planning ahead or privacy not being seen as significant as we might view them. Although majority Hindu, the Christian church has seen remarkable growth over the past few years.

What is the SRT project?

The Church of Scotland established the SRT Project in 1970 as it could see that technology has a profound, and sometimes unexpected, influence on many of our interactions. The church also appreciated the importance of the fact that people of faith have both the opportunity and the responsibility to engage in informed debate around these issues.

Recommended reading

In the BRF Lent book for 2020, David Walker explores different aspects of human belonging through the medium of scripture and story in order to help us recognise the different ways in which we are God's beloved. And as we recognise ourselves and our own lives in the narrative of God's engagement with humanity and his creation, he gently challenges us to engage for God's sake with God's world.

The following is an edited extract from a reading in the first week, entitled 'Jesus the teacher'.

BRF LENT BOOK

You Are Mine

Daily Bible readings from
Ash Wednesday to Easter Day

DAVID WALKER

I can still picture the faces of many of those who have taught me. Each in their way has influenced not only what I know but also what I value and how I behave. A sixth-form maths teacher instilled in me a desire not just to find the right answer but to get there by the most elegant and simple route. A university lecturer kindled in me a love for the most abstract of concepts. A college tutor helped me to develop confidence in myself as a public speaker. What's more, that practice of having a teacher who guides and inspires me didn't end when I knelt before a bishop to be ordained; it continued through the more experienced clergy with whom I worked in my early adult years, through to the diocesan bishop who was my first colleague after my own episcopal consecration and on to the professor who leads the group of scholars with which I do much of my theological research and reflection. To have a teacher is not to lack confidence in my own capabilities and experience, but it is to realise that I am still learning.

The title of teacher, or rabbi, is applied to Jesus a lot in the gospels. As with my own experience, it means much more than someone who imparts information. In fact, there is little suggestion that Jesus followed the widespread tradition of teaching his disciples large chunks of material that they then had to recite back to him accurately. We only have one prayer that he appears to have taught them to use. And even the Lord's Prayer itself reads more like an example or an outline around which anyone can build their own particular petitions.

Rather, the disciples accompanied Jesus from place to place as he ministered and were increasingly invited and entrusted to prepare the ground in the towns and villages he intended to visit. With greater or lesser degrees of success, during his earthly ministry and afterwards, they copied the kinds of things they had seen him doing. They took on the values that he espoused and demonstrated the love and forgiveness that lay at the heart of his teaching. Through this they became the community that began the process of converting large chunks of humanity to become his followers too.

At the heart of this lay the fact that he had never actually stopped being their teacher. Before his crucifixion, he had assured them, as recorded in John's gospel, that he would dwell within them. Matthew tells us that Jesus' final meeting with his disciples after his resurrection contained a promise to be with them until the end of the age. Jesus was true to his word. He went on being their teacher, and Christians around the world find him exercising that same role in their lives today.

A few years ago there was a fashion, especially among teenage Christians, for wearing a plastic wristband with the letters WWJD on it. The initials stood for 'What would Jesus do?' and were a simple invitation for the wearer to imagine how Christ would respond to the situation they were in before they fixed on a course of action. The fashion was treated by some with disdain. It was alleged to be simplistic, not least by seeking to find a direct answer from Jesus to a situation that could never have occurred during his earthly ministry. Nevertheless, I believe a great truth lies at its heart. If Jesus is our teacher, and we belong with him in at relationship as his first disciples did, then like them we should seek to copy his behaviour, even if that requires an effort of imaginative prayer rather than direct observation.

Moreover, that attempt to imagine the action and reaction of Jesus in a particular situation takes place in a much wider context. The Christian who takes Christ as teacher is seeking to follow the pattern of his teaching and the example of his life, not just in response to some isolated ethical dilemma but day in and day out. Through the imitation of Christ, a discipline that goes back down the centuries, we are slowly but surely transformed into his image, just as in the ancient world the goal of many a pupil was to become ever more like their master. As we grow in the likeness of Jesus, the work of behaving as he would becomes ever more natural to us, sustained by repetition as well as by our abiding relationship with him in each present moment.

> *Come Lord Jesus,*
> *and be our teacher,*
> *as you taught the people of Israel long ago.*
> *May we so follow your good example*
> *that we grow ever more in your likeness,*
> *until we take our place in heaven. Amen*

To order a copy of this book, please use the order form on page 149 or visit **brfonline.org.uk***.*

Servant Ministry
A portrait of Christ and a pattern for his followers
Tony Horsfall

A Fruitful Life
Abiding in Christ as seen in John 15
Tony Horsfall
Foreword by Steve Brady

An exposition of the first 'Servant Song' in Isaiah, *Servant Ministry* applies insights from that passage to topics such as the call to serve, valid expressions of servanthood, and the link between evangelism and social action.

Servant Ministry
A portrait of Christ and a pattern for his followers
Tony Horsfall
978 0 85746 886 4 £8.99
brfonline.org.uk

A Fruitful Life ponders the famous 'vine' passage of John 15. Just as Jesus' teaching transformed the lives of the first disciples, so a proper understanding of what he is saying can revolutionise our lives also.

A Fruitful Life
Abiding in Christ as seen in John 15
Tony Horsfall
978 0 85746 884 0 £8.99
brfonline.org.uk

Tony Horsfall and Debbie Hawker encourage us to develop our resilience and to prepare ourselves for the challenges that life throws at us in an increasingly difficult world. Through biblical wisdom and psychological insight, they show us how to understand ourselves better, appreciate our areas of strength and strengthen our areas of weakness. Read this book if you want a faith that persists to the finishing line.

Resilience in Life and Faith
Finding your strength in God
Tony Horsfall and Debbie Hawker
978 0 85746 734 8 £9.99
brfonline.org.uk

AVAILABLE NOW: **NEW HOLY HABITS** RESOURCES

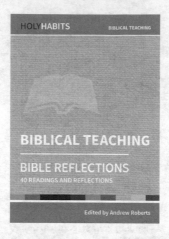

Holy Habits is an adventure in Christian discipleship. Inspired by Luke's model of church found in Acts 2:42–47, it identifies ten habits and encourages the development of a way of life formed by them.

Building on the Holy Habits resources published at the start of 2019, these Bible Reflections and Group Study materials are designed to help small groups and individuals build Holy Habits through Bible reading and group discussion questions. Easy to use, from a variety of different contributors, these booklets are the perfect addition to help your church's Holy Habits journey to thrive and flourish.

Holy Habits Bible Reflections
Edited by Andrew Roberts
£3.99

Holy Habits Group Studies
Edited by Andrew Roberts
£6.99

Available February 2020:
BREAKING BREAD | SHARING RESOURCES | SERVING |
GLADNESS AND GENEROSITY | WORSHIP

Find out more at brfonline.org.uk/holy-habits

Really Useful Guides

Each Really Useful Guide focuses on a specific biblical book, making it come to life for the reader, enabling them to understand the message and to apply its truth to today's circumstances. Though not a commentary, it gives valuable insight into the book's message. Though not an introduction, it summarises the important aspects of the book to aid reading and application.

Genesis 1—11
Rebecca Watson
978 0 85746 791 1 £5.99

Psalms
Simon P. Stock
978 0 85746 731 7 £6.99

John
Robert Willoughby
978 0 85746 751 5 £5.99

Colossians and Philemon
Derek Tidball
978 0 85746 730 0 £5.99

brfonline.org.uk

To order

Online: **brfonline.org.uk**
Telephone: +44 (0)1865 319700
Mon–Fri 9.15–17.30

Delivery times within the UK are
normally 15 working days. Prices are
correct at the time of going to press
but may change without prior notice.

Title	Price	Qty	Total
Life with St Benedict	£9.99		
Make the Most of Retirement	£7.99		
BRF Lent Book: You Are Mine	£8.99		
Servant Ministry	£8.99		
A Fruitful Life	£8.99		
Resilience in Life and Faith	£9.99		
Really Useful Guides: Gen 1–11 / John / Col & Phm* (*delete as appropriate)	£5.99		
Really Useful Guide: Psalms	£6.99		

POSTAGE AND PACKING CHARGES			
Order value	UK	Europe	Rest of world
Under £7.00	£2.00	Available on request	Available on request
£7.00–£29.99	£3.00		
£30.00 and over	FREE		

Total value of books	
Postage and packing	
Total for this order	

Please complete in BLOCK CAPITALS

Title _____ First name/initials _____ Surname _____

Address _____

_____ Postcode _____

Acc. No. _____ Telephone _____

Email _____

Method of payment

❏ Cheque (made payable to BRF) ❏ MasterCard / Visa

Card no. ▢▢▢▢ ▢▢▢▢ ▢▢▢▢ ▢▢▢▢

Expires end ▢▢ M M ▢▢ Y Y Security code* ▢▢▢   Last 3 digits on the reverse of the card

Signature* _____ Date _____ / _____ / _____
*ESSENTIAL IN ORDER TO PROCESS YOUR ORDER

Please return this form to:
BRF, 15 The Chambers, Vineyard, Abingdon OX14 3FE | enquiries@brf.org.uk
To read our terms and find out about cancelling your order, please visit brfonline.org.uk/terms.

The Bible Reading Fellowship (BRF) is a Registered Charity (233280)

How to encourage Bible reading in your church

BRF has been helping individuals connect with the Bible for over 90 years. We want to support churches as they seek to encourage church members into regular Bible reading.

Order a Bible reading resources pack

This pack is designed to give your church the tools to publicise our Bible reading notes. It includes:

- Sample Bible reading notes for your congregation to try.
- Publicity resources, including a poster.
- A church magazine feature about Bible reading notes.

The pack is free, but we welcome a £5 donation to cover the cost of postage. If you require a pack to be sent outside the UK or require a specific number of sample Bible reading notes, please contact us for postage costs.

How to order and find out more

- Email **enquiries@brf.org.uk**
- Telephone BRF on +44 (0)1865 319700 Mon–Fri 9.15–17.30
- Write to us at BRF, 15 The Chambers, Vineyard, Abingdon OX14 3FE

Keep informed about our latest initiatives

We are continuing to develop resources to help churches encourage people into regular Bible reading, wherever they are on their journey. Join our email list at **brfonline.org.uk** to stay informed about the latest initiatives that your church could benefit from.

Transforming lives and communities

BRF is a charity that is passionate about making a difference through the Christian faith. We want to see lives and communities transformed through our creative programmes and resources for individuals, churches and schools. We are doing this by resourcing:

- **Christian growth and understanding of the Bible.** Through our Bible reading notes, books, digital resources, Holy Habits, conferences and other events, we're resourcing individuals, groups and leaders in churches for their own spiritual journey and for their ministry.

- **Church outreach in the local community.** BRF is the home of two programmes that churches are embracing to great effect as they seek to engage with their local communities: Messy Church and Anna Chaplaincy.

- **Teaching Christianity in primary schools.** Our Barnabas in Schools team is working with primary-aged children and their teachers, enabling them to explore Christianity creatively and confidently within the school curriculum.

- **Children's and family ministry.** Through our Parenting for Faith programme, websites and published resources, we're working with churches and families, enabling children and adults alike to explore Christianity creatively and bring the Bible alive.

Do you share our vision?

Sales of our books and Bible reading notes cover the cost of producing them. However, our other programmes are funded primarily by donations, grants and legacies. If you share our vision, would you help us to transform even more lives and communities? Your prayers and financial support are vital for the work that we do. You could:

- support BRF's ministry with a regular donation (at **brf.org.uk/donate**);
- support us with a one off gift (use the form on pages 153–54);
- consider leaving a gift to BRF in your will (see page 152);
- encourage your church to support BRF as part of your church's giving to home mission – perhaps focusing on a specific area of our ministry, or a particular member of our Barnabas in Schools team.
- most important of all, support BRF with your prayers.

Help us raise God-connected children and teens through a gift in your will

Aged twelve, Jesus went with his family to Jerusalem to celebrate the Feast of Passover. After the festival, the family began their journey home, but Jesus was not among them. He stayed behind 'in the temple courts, sitting among the teachers, listening to them and asking them questions' (Luke 2:46, NIV).

It's a picture that may sound familiar to some parents. Perhaps you can remember a time when you were trying to get your kids ready for school, a family meal or another engagement. There was much to do and time was slipping away, but all your kids wanted to do was ask questions about anything and everything.

As a parent you often want to encourage your children to ask questions, spiritual or otherwise, so that they can learn and discover new things. But life must go on and those shoe laces won't tie themselves! It's a tricky predicament.

Our Parenting for Faith team understands this dichotomy. They aim to equip parents and carers to confidently parent for faith in the midst of the mundane: when ferrying the children back and forth, sitting on the bathroom floor potty training toddlers or waving kids off on their first day of secondary school.

Through their website, an eight-session course and numerous events and training opportunities, the Parenting for Faith team are helping Christian parents raise God-connected children and teens. They're helping to raise a new generation that can bring God's love to a world in need.

Could you help this work continue by leaving a gift in your will? Even a small amount can help make a lasting difference in the lives of parents and children.

For further information about making a gift to BRF in your will, please visit **brf.org.uk/lastingdifference**, contact us at **+44 (0)1865 319700** or email **giving@brf.org.uk**.

Whatever you can do or give, we thank you for your support.

Pray. Give. Get involved.
brf.org.uk

SHARING OUR VISION – MAKING A GIFT

I would like to make a gift to support BRF. Please use my gift for:

☐ where it is needed most ☐ Barnabas in Schools ☐ Parenting for Faith
☐ Messy Church ☐ Anna Chaplaincy

Title	First name/initials	Surname

Address

Postcode

Email

Telephone

Signature	Date

giftaid it You can add an extra 25p to every £1 you give.

Please treat as Gift Aid donations all qualifying gifts of money made

☐ today, ☐ in the past four years, ☐ and in the future.

I am a UK taxpayer and understand that if I pay less Income Tax and/or Capital Gains Tax in the current tax year than the amount of Gift Aid claimed on all my donations, it is my responsibility to pay any difference.

☐ My donation does not qualify for Gift Aid.

Please notify BRF if you want to cancel this Gift Aid declaration, change your name or home address, or no longer pay sufficient tax on your income and/or capital gains.

Please complete other side of form ➲

Please return this form to:
BRF, 15 The Chambers, Vineyard, Abingdon OX14 3FE

The Bible Reading Fellowship is a Registered Charity (233280)

SHARING OUR VISION – MAKING A GIFT

Regular giving

By Direct Debit: You can set up a Direct Debit quickly and easily
at **brf.org.uk/donate**

By Standing Order: Please contact our Fundraising Administrator
+44 (0)1865 319700 | **giving@brf.org.uk**

One-off donation

Please accept my gift of:

☐ £10 ☐ £50 ☐ £100 Other £ ☐

by (*delete as appropriate*):

☐ Cheque/Charity Voucher payable to 'BRF'

☐ MasterCard/Visa/Debit card/Charity card

Name on card

Card no. ☐☐☐☐ ☐☐☐☐ ☐☐☐☐ ☐☐☐☐

Expires end ☐☐ ☐☐ Security code* ☐☐☐

*Last 3 digits on the reverse of the card
ESSENTIAL IN ORDER TO PROCESS
YOUR PAYMENT

Signature   Date

☐ I would like to leave a gift in my will to BRF.

For more information, visit **brf.org.uk/lastingdifference**

For help or advice regarding making a gift, please contact our Fundraising
Administrator +44 (0)1865 319700

🡐 Please complete other side of form

Please return this form to:
BRF, 15 The Chambers, Vineyard, Abingdon OX14 3FE

BRF

The Bible Reading Fellowship is a Registered Charity (233280)

NEW DAYLIGHT SUBSCRIPTION RATES

Please note our new subscription rates, current until 30 April 2021:

Individual subscriptions
covering 3 issues for under 5 copies, payable in advance
(including postage & packing):

	UK	Europe	Rest of world
New Daylight	£17.85	£25.80	£29.70
New Daylight 3-year subscription (9 issues) (not available for Deluxe)	£50.85	N/A	N/A
New Daylight Deluxe per set of 3 issues p.a.	£22.35	£32.55	£38.55

Group subscriptions
covering 3 issues for 5 copies or more, sent to one UK address (post free):

New Daylight	£14.10 per set of 3 issues p.a.
New Daylight Deluxe	£17.85 per set of 3 issues p.a.

Please note that the annual billing period for group subscriptions runs from 1 May to 30 April.

Overseas group subscription rates
Available on request. Please email **enquiries@brf.org.uk**.

Copies may also be obtained from Christian bookshops:

New Daylight	£4.70 per copy
New Daylight Deluxe	£5.95 per copy

All our Bible reading notes can be ordered online by visiting
brfonline.org.uk/collections/subscriptions

New Daylight is also available as an app for
Android, iPhone and iPad
brfonline.org.uk/collections/apps

NEW DAYLIGHT INDIVIDUAL SUBSCRIPTION FORM

All our Bible reading notes can be ordered online by visiting
brfonline.org.uk/collections/subscriptions

☐ I would like to take out a subscription:

Title _____ First name/initials _____ Surname _____

Address _____

_____ Postcode _____

Telephone _____ Email _____

Please send *New Daylight* beginning with the May 2020 / September 2020 /
January 2021 issue (*delete as appropriate*):

(please tick box)	UK	Europe	Rest of world
New Daylight 1-year subscription	☐ £17.85	☐ £25.80	☐ £29.70
New Daylight 3-year subscription	☐ £50.85	N/A	N/A
New Daylight Deluxe	☐ £22.35	☐ £32.55	☐ £38.55

Total enclosed £ _____ (cheques should be made payable to 'BRF')

Please charge my MasterCard / Visa ☐ Debit card ☐ with £ _____

Card no. ☐☐☐☐ ☐☐☐☐ ☐☐☐☐ ☐☐☐☐

Expires end ☐☐ ☐☐   Security code* ☐☐☐   Last 3 digits on the reverse of the card

Signature* _____ Date _____ /_____ /_____
*ESSENTIAL IN ORDER TO PROCESS YOUR PAYMENT

To set up a Direct Debit, please also complete the Direct Debit instruction on page 159
and return it to BRF with this form.

Please return this form with the appropriate payment to:
BRF, 15 The Chambers, Vineyard, Abingdon OX14 3FE

To read our terms and find out about cancelling your order,
please visit **brfonline.org.uk/terms**.

The Bible Reading Fellowship is a Registered Charity (233280)

ND0120

NEW DAYLIGHT GIFT SUBSCRIPTION FORM

☐ I would like to give a gift subscription (please provide both names and addresses):

Title .... First name/initials .... Surname ....

Address ....

.... Postcode ....

Telephone .... Email ....

Gift subscription name ....

Gift subscription address ....

.... Postcode ....

Gift message (20 words max. or include your own gift card):

....

....

Please send *New Daylight* beginning with the May 2020 / September 2020 / January 2021 issue (*delete as appropriate*):

(*please tick box*)	UK	Europe	Rest of world
New Daylight 1-year subscription	☐ £17.85	☐ £25.80	☐ £29.70
New Daylight 3-year subscription	☐ £50.85	N/A	N/A
New Daylight Deluxe	☐ £22.35	☐ £32.55	☐ £38.55

Total enclosed £ .... (cheques should be made payable to 'BRF')

Please charge my MasterCard / Visa ☐ Debit card ☐ with £ ....

Card no. ☐☐☐☐ ☐☐☐☐ ☐☐☐☐ ☐☐☐☐

Expires end ☐☐☐☐ Security code* ☐☐☐ Last 3 digits on the reverse of the card

Signature* .... Date ...... /...... /......

*ESSENTIAL IN ORDER TO PROCESS YOUR PAYMENT

To set up a Direct Debit, please also complete the Direct Debit instruction on page 159 and return it to BRF with this form.

Please return this form with the appropriate payment to:
BRF, 15 The Chambers, Vineyard, Abingdon OX14 3FE

To read our terms and find out about cancelling your order, please visit **brfonline.org.uk/terms**.

The Bible Reading Fellowship is a Registered Charity (233280)

DIRECT DEBIT PAYMENT

You can pay for your annual subscription to our Bible reading notes using Direct Debit. You need only give your bank details once, and the payment is made automatically every year until you cancel it. If you would like to pay by Direct Debit, please use the form opposite, entering your BRF account number under 'Reference number'.

You are fully covered by the Direct Debit Guarantee:

The Direct Debit Guarantee

- This Guarantee is offered by all banks and building societies that accept instructions to pay Direct Debits.

- If there are any changes to the amount, date or frequency of your Direct Debit, The Bible Reading Fellowship will notify you 10 working days in advance of your account being debited or as otherwise agreed. If you request The Bible Reading Fellowship to collect a payment, confirmation of the amount and date will be given to you at the time of the request.

- If an error is made in the payment of your Direct Debit, by The Bible Reading Fellowship or your bank or building society, you are entitled to a full and immediate refund of the amount paid from your bank or building society.

- If you receive a refund you are not entitled to, you must pay it back when The Bible Reading Fellowship asks you to.

- You can cancel a Direct Debit at any time by simply contacting your bank or building society. Written confirmation may be required. Please also notify us.

The Bible Reading Fellowship

Instruction to your bank or building society to pay by Direct Debit

Please fill in the whole form using a ballpoint pen and return it to:
BRF, 15 The Chambers, Vineyard, Abingdon OX14 3FE

Service User Number: | 5 | 5 | 8 | 2 | 2 | 9 |

Name and full postal address of your bank or building society

To: The Manager	Bank/Building Society
Address	
	Postcode

Name(s) of account holder(s)

Branch sort code

| | | – | | | – | | | |

Bank/Building Society account number

| | | | | | | | | |

Reference number

| | | | | | | | |

Instruction to your Bank/Building Society
Please pay The Bible Reading Fellowship Direct Debits from the account detailed in this instruction, subject to the safeguards assured by the Direct Debit Guarantee. I understand that this instruction may remain with The Bible Reading Fellowship and, if so, details will be passed electronically to my bank/building society.

Signature(s)

Banks and Building Societies may not accept Direct Debit instructions for some types of account.

BRF

Transforming
lives and communities

Christian growth and understanding of the Bible

Resourcing individuals, groups and leaders in churches for their own spiritual journey and for their ministry

Church outreach in the local community

Offering two programmes that churches are embracing to great effect as they seek to engage with their local communities and transform lives

Teaching Christianity in primary schools

Working with children and teachers to explore Christianity creatively and confidently

Children's and family ministry

Working with churches and families to explore Christianity creatively and bring the Bible alive

parenting for faith

Visit **brf.org.uk** for more information on BRF's work

brf.org.uk